"This is a wonderful book. Informative and intriguing. *Networking Magic* will change your life."

—John Gray, Ph.D., author of
Men Are from Mars, Women Are from Venus

"Read this GREAT book and you'll learn how to make extraordinary contacts that will forever change and improve your life."

—Mark Victor Hansen, creator of the
Chicken Soup for the Soul series

"Networking will change your life . . . and this book will get you started!"

—Harvey Mackay, author of the #1 *New York Times* bestseller
Swim with the Sharks Without Being Eaten Alive

"An absolute winner! Explains how to get it all by networking. A gem on how to build and maintain relationships! Will enrich your life. Not just the ABCs of networking, *Networking Magic* is the whole alphabet."

—Herb Cohen, author of *You Can Negotiate Anything*
and *Negotiate This*

"*Networking Magic* is pure magic, it opened my eyes. A great informative book! I learned tons from it! Finally, a great information-packed book that says it ALL about networking. Destined to become the networker's bible; breezy, easy to read and information-packed—I thought I knew networking until I read this amazing book! Frishman and Lublin know networking. Read *Networking Magic* and you will too. The new, must-read classic on networking. Don't leave home without it!"

—Jack Canfield, coauthor *Chicken Soup for the Soul* series
and CEO of Chicken Soup for the Soul Enterprises

"*Networking Magic* teaches an important principle: that by connecting with and serving others, you also serve yourself. As the authors put it, 'Generosity is the soul of networking.'"

—Ken Blanchard, coauthor of *The One Minute Manager* and
The Leadership Pill

"You have to build relationships to be successful today, and *Networking Magic* will show you how to do just that. My one complaint is that this book was not available when I started my business career!"

—Jim McCann, CEO, 1-800-FLOWERS.COM

"*Networking Magic* is pure magic! From page one, it reads quickly and clearly teaches you how to improve every aspect of your life."

—Les Brown, motivational speaker and author of
Live Your Dreams and *Up Thoughts For Down Times*

"*Networking Magic* transforms the invisible ingredients for success into visible, viable and practical action steps. Nobody does it better than Rick and Jill. They have taught me 'unless you are networking you soon will be not working!'"

—Dr. Denis Waitley, author of *The Seeds of Greatness*

"Frishman and Lublin have done it again! In *Networking Magic* they reveal the secrets and insights of successful networkers in a manner that is easy and fun to read."

—Robin Sharma, author of *The Monk Who Sold His Ferrari* and
The Saint, the Surfer and the CEO

"From A to Z, *Networking Magic* includes everything you need to know about networking. It's an indispensable book. I wish I'd had a copy when I started publishing twelve years ago!"

—Gregory J. P. Godek, author of *1001 Ways to Be Romantic*

"Make this book your desk bible on how to make positive connections every time you step out of your office and into the marketplace. Your networking strategy will come alive!"

—Mark LeBlanc, author of *Growing Your Business!*

"*Networking Magic*'s simple tools and amazing insights inspire others to help you. It is the 'how-to' on achieving success."

—Romanus Wolter, "The Kick Start Guy"

"This book brings as much spirit and value to your business acumen as Jill Lublin and Rick Frishman add to your personal network. Do yourself a favor by reading their generous and thoughtful book! A great read about a critical and often ignored discipline in business and in life."

—Tom Ehrenfeld, author of *The Startup Garden:*
How Growing a Business Grows You
(www.startupgarden.com)

"If you want to build successful relationships with others, this book is for you. This book will help you to discover the dynamics of how to make networking work effectively for YOU. Building relationships and creating lots of shameless fans has helped me to grow my business faster than any other marketing strategy I've tried. This book will show you how to be a master at it!"

—Debbie Allen, award-winning author of
Confessions of Shameless Self Promoters
(www.confessionsofshameless.com)

"Networking is a master skill in business and life. This book will show you how to master the art of networking!"

—Sam Silverstein, CSP (Certified Speaking Professional)

"*Networking Magic* is exactly the right book at the right time for anyone trying to get ahead. Frishman and Lublin clearly demonstrate 'It's who you know' when it comes to nearly any type of success. If you follow their first-rate easy to understand practical advice you'll soon know everyone!"

—Steven Schragis, National Director, Learning Annex

"The inside secrets of two networking pros. In *Networking Magic*, Frishman and Lublin teach you how to build and maintain powerful networks that will get you on top and keep you there."

—Robert Allen, coauthor of *The One-Minute Millionaire*

"The special tactics covered in this book are absolute gems. Here you'll discover a foolproof system for remembering names and many super networking strategies that outperform any other method. Buy it! You won't be sorry."

—Marilyn Ross, author of *Shameless Marketing for Brazen Hussies* and eleven other books *(Marilyn@MarilynRoss.com)*

"There is a lot more to life than just 'showing up.' Frishman and Lublin's new book will make sure that you know how to show up at the right time and place, and meet the right group of people. If networking is important to you, reading this book and heeding its simple, smart advice is the first step you should take."

—Stephen Burgay, Senior Vice President/Corporate Communications, John Hancock Financial Services

"Authors and publishers network freely. We do not compete: Since every book is unique, no one feels threatened. This book shows book people how to help each other even more effectively."

—Dan Poynter, author of *The Self-Publishing Manual* *(www.parapublishing.com)*

"If you're fishing for better contacts and bigger business, Lublin and Frishman will expertly show you how to hook those connections and make the magic happen!"

—Randy Peyser, bestselling author of
Crappy to Happy: Small Steps to Big Happiness NOW!
(www.crappytohappy.com)

"If you plan to deal with people—at any level—don't make a move without reading *Networking Magic*. It's full of great information and amazing insights on a subject we all need to master."

—Mike Fink, International NLP Trainer, Speaker and Consultant,
Founder of Magician Within, Inc.

"To succeed today, you must be a great networker and *Networking Magic* will show you the way. It's the best, most comprehensive and practical book on networking."

—Bill Lauterbach of FIVE STAR Speakers & Trainers, LLC

"*Networking Magic* gives you everything you need to know about networking, and didn't know to ask. In turbulent, fast changing times, you lose if you aren't a savvy schmoozer. This book is a definite Keeper!"

—Dr. Judith Briles, author of
The Confidence Factor
(www.Briles.com)

"All of marketing, all of business, can be broken down to one thing: creating relationships—or, as I like to put it, making friends. If you haven't figured out how to make friends yet, read *Networking Magic*. It could change your life in a very good way."

—John Kremer, author of *1001 Ways to Market Your Books*

"If any two people can create networking magic, it's Rick Frishman and Jill Lublin. Being in the communications field myself, I know artists when I see them. When it comes to expanding your 'list' and getting the most out of it, these two are artists."

—Joel Roberts, media consultant, former prime-time talk show host KABC Radio, Los Angeles

"Frishman and Lublin have done it—again. *Networking Magic* is like a tsunami of fresh air, chock-full of useful, bone-honest insights into a subject important to us all. Thank you for writing this book!"

—Bill Catlette, workforce guru and coauthor of *Contented Cows Give Better Milk*

"Clear, comprehensive and loaded with fabulous stories, *Networking Magic* is the networker's Bible. People will be talking about and using this remarkable new book for years."

—James F. Barry Jr., CFP, financial advisor, author, and host of PBS's *Jim Barry's Financial Success*

"I went from flight attendant to published author, by using the principles from *Networking Magic*! Thanks Rick and Jill!"

—Marsha Marks, author of *101 Simple Lessons for Life*

"A sure-fire networking classic! The fastest way to succeed is through the help of other people, and Frishman and Lublin divulge the secrets to uncommon success."

—Mike Litman, coauthor of *Conversations with Millionaires*

"Jill Lublin and Rick Frishman wisely point out that networking is ultimately about cultivating (and enjoying) the habit of insisting on someone else's success. And it's the only way to ensure that someone, somewhere will insist on yours. And that's where the magic comes in. Every time."

—Gail Blanke, CEO/President of Lifedesigns; author of *In My Wildest Dreams*

"Networking is the key to success in all realms of our lives. This book will jump-start you."

—Suzy Allegra, author of *How to Be Ageless: Growing Better, Not Just Older!*

"I love *Networking Magic*. The authors have raised the bar of networking to an art as they describe an enriching lifestyle rather than a series of tactics. The book is filled with gems—a 'must-read' to achieve greater success through building win-win relationships."

—Lynn Joseph, Ph.D., Career Transition Consultant and author of *The Job-Loss Recovery Guide: A Proven Program for Getting Back to Work—Fast!*

"Networking Magic is a must read. It contains an enormous variety of networking ideas, served up with anecdotes and stories that show exactly how they work. The book is dynamic, delightful and abundantly full of valuable, usable information."

—Angie Hollerich, CEP, CCA, owner, Brass Ring Productions, Ltd.; author of *The Weight and Wealth Factors*, *Grab the Brass Ring of Financial Security*, *The Wellness Path*, and *Tips from the Top*

"Human beings do networking, or connecting, naturally. *Networking Magic* is a fascinating study of how to do it with elegance, grace, generosity and success. This book will teach you how to do it to improve both your business and your personal life."

—Catherine Jewell, speaker and author of *STAR Performance*

"*Networking Magic* has everything you need to know about networking from A to Z. This book will help you attract clients and contacts with ease."

—Caterina Rando, M.A., MCC, speaker, trainer, and master coach; author of *Learn to Power Think*

"Jill Lublin and Rick Frishman are the greatest! Their generous advice and tremendous resources helped my company get the word out. Thank you both for your Magic!"

—Loral L. Langemeier, M.A., CPPC, founder/CEO of Live Out
Loud & WealthDiva.com

"This much-needed book is just the ticket for rejection-proofing your networking experiences."

—Elayne Savage, Ph.D., author of *Don't Take It Personally!* and
The Art of Dealing with Rejection

"This is Networking 101 at its best. It should be required reading by every business executive. An enriching, inspirational experience . . . it will change your business and personal relationship thinking."

—Hans Helmuth, CEO, NewBusinessNetwork.Biz

"Finally, a common-sense book with techniques everyone can use."

—Andrea Frank Henkart, author of *Cool Communication*

"*Networking Magic* is the magic bullet for business success."

—Cynthia Kersey, *Unstoppable*

"For over 75 years, Welcome Wagon has been providing a networking opportunity for local businesses and new homeowners. *Networking Magic* is the how-to guide for creating connections in today's hectic world."

—Greg Hebner, President, Welcome Wagon

Networking
Magic

Find the Best—
from Doctors, Lawyers, and Accountants
to Homes, Schools, and Jobs

Rick Frishman and Jill Lublin
with Mark Steisel

Adams Media
Avon, Massachusetts

To my wife Robbi, with love and thanks
—*Rick Frishman*

To God, who makes my life and light possible.
May I always spread great messages to make a difference
and serve the world. I am grateful for all your blessings.
—*Jill Lublin*

Published by
Adams Media, an F+W Publications Company
57 Littlefield Street, Avon, MA 02322. U.S.A.
www.adamsmedia.com

ISBN: 1-59337-020-2

Printed in the United States of America.

J I H G F E D C B

Library of Congress Cataloging-in-Publication Data
Frishman, Rick
Networking magic / by Rick Frishman and Jill Lublin, with Mark Steisel.
p.   cm.
ISBN 1-59337-020-2
1. Social networks. 2. Career development.
I. Lublin, Jill. II. Steisel, Mark. III. Title.
HM741F75 2004
302—dc22
2004002189

This publication is designed to provide accurate and authoritative information with
regard to the subject matter covered. It is sold with the understanding that the publisher is not engaged in rendering legal, accounting, or other professional advice. If
legal advice or other expert assistance is required, the services of a competent professional person should be sought.
—From a *Declaration of Principles* jointly adopted by a Committee of the American Bar Association and a Committee of Publishers and Associations

Many of the designations used by manufacturers and sellers to distinguish their
products are claimed as trademarks. Where those designations appear in this
book and Adams Media was aware of a trademark claim, the designations have
been printed with initial capital letters.

This book is available at quantity discounts for bulk purchases.
For information, call 1-800-872-5627.

Contents

Acknowledgments

This book is the direct product of networking. It owes its existence to the generous sharing of others, many of whom were strangers when we began this project. Virtually every word, idea, and suggestion that fills these pages were graciously given to us or reinforced by friends, friends of friends, friends of friend's friends, and so on. Tracing the linkage of all the connections is as hopeless as tracing your thoughts for the month.

We want to thank the people listed below who have made this book a reality. They gave us an outpouring of networking information and made the experience of writing this book magical. Scores of strangers became our collaborators and our friends. They told us their stories, revealed their secrets, and explained how their businesses, interests, and lives worked. They called us and spoke at length on their dime. They told their friends and contacts, who called us and did the same. They sent us FedEx packages stuffed with their books, promotional materials, audios, videos, and their thoughts. They gave and gave and gave.

People we never met invited us to dinners, to meetings, and conferences, and into their homes and lives. Many took the time to write long, detailed e-mails and happily answered all of our questions and follow-up calls. After we spoke, they contacted us to ask if we needed additional information and sent us thank-you notes. They continually gave far more than we asked or even expected, and were, and still are, willing to give even more. Our friends and collaborators not only gave us information, they also shared their secrets and allowed us to publish the fruits of their wisdom in a book we planned to sell.

A number of speakers and authors of networking books—including established and recognized authorities who could have considered us competitors—willingly provided their help. They showered us with information, stories, and quotes. Instead of treating us as rivals, they acted as if we were new kids in the community—the *networking* community. They welcomed us, mentored us, and seemed happy to show us the ropes. They didn't try to sell us or to impress us; they simply tried to help. We learned as much about networking from the manner in which they gave as we did from the invaluable information they disclosed. So to the following people, our friends and contributors, thanks for all of your amazing and generous help! We could not have written this book without you.

Frank Agin, Esq.	Jackie Hall
Mitch Axelrod	Mark Victor Hansen
Cherie Galloway Backus	C. J. Hayden
Connie Benesch	Angie Hollerich
Susan Benjamin	Jerry Horn
Jesse B'Franklin	Julia Hubbel
Randy Block	Robert Iger
Linda Breakeall	Jeff Kahn
Kenneth Browning, Esq.	Leonard Koren
Stephen Burgay	Steve Krauser
Adam Christing	Ian "Ike" Krieger
Dennis Crow	Brian Kurtz
Hellen Davis	Mark LeBlanc
Bernhard Dohrmann	Edward L. Lefkowitz
George DoLese	Robyn Levin
Marty Edelston	Steve Lillo
T. Harv Eker	Mike Litman
Dr. Stuart Fischer	Harvey Mackay
Rachel Frishman	Karen McCollough
Elissa Giambiastini	Sarah Michel
Ken Glickman	Jennifer Morla

Neil Mullanaphy
Andrea R. Nierenberg
Debra Pestrak
Randy Peyser
Robin Ramsey
Caterina Rando
Susan RoAne
Renee Wall Rongen
Paul Rosenzweig
Stanton Royce
Marta Salas-Porras
Darryl Salerno
Peter A. Schaible

Dave Sherman
Sara Slavin
Richard Solomon, Esq.
Barry Spilchuk
Marisa Thalberg
Larry Turell
Robert Turell
Melissa Wahl
Marlena Weinstein
Kym Yancy
Sandra Yancy
James Ziegler

On a personal note, my first thank you goes to my wonderful co-author Jill Lublin. And to Mark Steisel—your help and wisdom have been invaluable. Working with both of you has been a joy.

Thank you to our super editor at Adams Media, Jill Alexander; and to Gary Krebs and, of course, the man who made this happen . . . Scott Watrous. Thank you, Beth Gissinger, publicity guru at Adams for all of your hard work, and to Amy Collins, saleswoman extraordinaire.

I have to acknowledge Mike (Manny) Levine, who founded Planned Television Arts in 1962 and was my mentor and partner for over eighteen years. Mike taught me that work has to be fun and meaningful and then the profits will follow.

Thanks to my exceptional management team at PTA: David Hahn, David Thalberg, and Sandy Trupp. Your professionalism, loyalty, and friendship mean more to me than you will ever know. To the staff of PTA: You are the best in the business.

Thank you to David and Peter Finn, Tony Esposito, Richard Funess, and all of my colleagues at Ruder Finn. It is an honor to be part of this amazing company.

To my friends Mark Victor Hansen and Jack Canfield:

Making the journey with the two of you has been incredible, and your friendship and advice has been invaluable.

To Harvey Mackay: For the lessons about networking and for your amazing support. You are in a class of your own.

Thanks also to my mother and father, for keeping me out of the fur business and helping me discover my own destiny. And to my brother Scott, who has always been there to support me in whatever I do.

To my children Adam, Rachel, and Stephanie: Watching you grow into fine young individuals is the highlight of my life. And to my wife Robbi—you are my strength.

—Rick Frishman

I so appreciate my coauthor—Rick Frishman, a brilliant colleague and terrific collaborator, and I acknowledge with deep gratitude the efforts and superb work of Mark Steisel, a man who turns dreams into reality! Thanks to the super people at Adams Media—Jill Alexander, our incredible, talented, and committed editor; and the leading men, Gary Krebs and Scott Watrous. Thank you for making this happen! Beth Gissinger, thank you for publicizing the publicists.

I appreciate, love, and acknowledge my parents, Rose Wolfenson and Seymour Lublin. Thank you for birthing and loving me into the person I am. Steve Lillo—a partner beyond my dreams—your continuous, unending, unconditional love, and support provide a rock-solid foundation for my life.

I also want to acknowledge the varied contributions of so many colleagues, mentors, and friends. Thank you one and all:

- Patricia and Vern McDade, the creators of the Entrepreneurial Edge who taught me possibility with a "capital P." I thank you and bless you for your teaching. I also want to acknowledge your outrageously dedicated staff and incredible coaches: Susan James, Mike Altman, K. Marie Lim, Lauretta Hayes, Kim Altman, Caryn Condon, Susan Harmon, Bill Rogers, Yvonne Teruya, Ralph White, Michele-Joy DelRe, and the whole family of community and colleagues who have enriched my life for many years.

- Income Builders International Global (IBI Global, Inc.)— the circle of angels, friends, and dream team builders— particularly, Lynn Dohrmann (president) and Berny Dohrmann (founder), two visionaries committed to growing dreams and businesses.

- Mark LeBlanc, whose superb advice, incredible support, and sweet heart have contributed greatly to my life and success.

- The staff of Promising Promotion & GoodNews Media.net, past and present, who have contributed their work, dedication, and passion. Jennifer Geronimo, you are a beacon for me and I am grateful for who you are in my life.

- Michelle Rochwarger—a dear friend whose profound business advice and friendship means the world.

And, finally, thanks to my amazing friends, coaches, and family who bring such support, heart, joy, direction, advice, spirit, and sweetness into my life: Randy Peyser, Carole Kramer, Jeff Herzbach, Marie Cooke, Misha Henckel, Taron Puri, Eliot Kahn, Les Hewitt, T. Haru Eker, Andrea and Reggie Henkart, David and Andrea Lieberstein, Jay Conrad Levinson, Michael Larsen, Elizabeth Pomada, Loral Langemeier, Mitch Santell, Hollis Polk, Lynn Kulsar, Marjorie Stark, Vince Delgado, Carol Heller, Jessica Heller Frank, Steve Lublin and family, Jack Lublin, Lynn Fox and family, Caterina Rando, Francine Ward, Shaari Kamil, Gloria Wilcox, Tina Varela, Camille Kurtz, and all my other angels and guides on this marvelous life journey, both visible and invisible.

—*Jill Lublin*

Foreword

Work life today is increasingly hectic. Since the advent of the Internet and the invention of cell phones, the way we communicate and interact with coworkers and friends has changed drastically. When Monster was founded in 1994, the idea of using the Internet to find a job was considered impractical—many critics thought it wouldn't catch on. Instead, Monster revolutionized the way job seekers and employers connect and forever changed how people make connections in their professional life. And since networking is an essential part of not only finding a job but also doing a job well, we launched Monster Networking so that professionals across all industries and levels can exchange information about jobs, offer expertise, and help others achieve their goals.

Although our methods of communication have multiplied exponentially, finding connections with our peers, neighbors, and friends within our community has become increasingly elusive. Strategies for networking have changed with the times. As a professional, you need a game plan for building and maintaining relationships with your network of friends, colleagues, and peers. Brimming with savvy insights, fun anecdotes, and practical tips, *Networking Magic* gives you the top strategies for finding the best resources and opportunities.

So many people think of networking as schmoozing or manipulating others. Rick and Jill understand that networking isn't about taking—it's about showing up. This book does a wonderful job of demonstrating how integral networking is to our lives. If you want to get something done, you need other people to help you. This book will help you realize that those people are all around you. *Networking Magic* is a great book. Too bad it wasn't written twenty years ago—it would have saved me a lot of work!

—*Michael Schutzler,*
SVP, Consumer Products, Monster Worldwide

Introduction

A number of recent publications have heralded networking as the new wonder drug that will enable you to thrive in either a slumping or a booming economy. They give the impression that by following a few relatively easy steps—presto!—you can propel the smallest, most obscure business straight to the top of the *Fortune* 500 list. Or that you can use networking to meet the perfect partner, get the ideal job, or otherwise strike the mother lode.

First, let's clarify that networking isn't new. It's an essential part of human interaction. Until recently networking was referred to as being "well connected," or having "contacts" or a great Rolodex. It's something we've heard about all of our lives, though it's been referred to in different ways or with different buzzwords. Whenever someone recommends a restaurant, a travel agent, or a book, that's networking. Networking isn't new and it isn't some miraculous potion that you can gulp down before bedtime to cure whatever ails you by the next morning.

Undeniably, networking is a valuable tool. Reports claim that over 80 percent of all jobs are obtained through networking. Clearly, networking can boost sales and increase profits. It can help you find a wonderful place to live, a great caterer, and an endless stream of professional services.

Getting the Very Best

The purpose of this book is to teach you how to build and maintain networks that will help you get the BEST: the best doctor, lawyer, job, sweetheart, partner, client, auto mechanic, and so on. Our premise is that we all have network contacts and by adjusting our focus slightly, we can position ourselves to get the very best. Shooting for the best has endless benefits, which include distinguishing you from the competition, impressing others, and more quickly helping you to reach your goals. Plus, it will bring greater stimulation, excitement, and satisfaction to your life.

To get the best, you must surround yourself with the most outstanding, caring, and helpful people. You must build mutually supportive relationships with top people who will happily help you and who have what it takes to satisfy your needs.

Networking is more than a career, a marketing gimmick, or social tactic—it's a way of life. And it doesn't occur overnight! New York attorney Richard Solomon put it best when he said, "The object in life is to be rich in the resource of people." And we agree! Nothing is more important or will enrich your life as greatly as forging close personal relationships, which is what networking provides. And it gets even better when those relationships are with the best and most outstanding people! What could be sweeter than only dealing with the best?

Our Stories

We decided to write this book because networking has been such a central and integral part of our lives. Through networking we have been fortunate enough to forge close relationships that have helped us rise to the top of our profession and that have made our personal lives full and rewarding. Networking has helped us realize our dreams. Through networking we have met, worked, and socialized with extraordinary people who have enriched our lives in ways we never imagined.

Since our experiences and good fortune are so intertwined with networking, we want to share the lessons we have learned. It is our way of saying "thanks" for all the help we have received, of giving back and helping others better their lives. We believe that we are uniquely qualified to write this book because we have built and maintained our careers through strong network relationships.

Rick's Story

Every part of my life is networking. I met my wife at a party I was invited to by a friend. Practically everyone who works for my company got their job through someone I know. My personal life revolves around networking, and I base most of my decisions on the recommendations I get from friends.

My first job came through networking. I had just graduated from Ithaca College, with no prospects, when a high school friend told me that the *Barry Farber Radio Show* needed a producer. She gave me the name of the person to contact. At Farber, I got to know Mike Levine, the founder of the public relations firm Planned Television Arts, who called frequently to try to publicize his clients' books. Mike offered me a job and when I joined PTA, we had just a few clients. To build the business, I asked everyone I knew to give me three names of people I could call. From those contacts and their referrals, we built a huge client list.

When Mike Levine decided to retire, I threw a combination retirement and thirtieth anniversary party for PTA. I invited a friend of my father who was the chairman of a large PR firm. When he got the invitation he called me and said, "There's good news and bad news. I can't come to your party, but I want to buy your company."

We entered into negotiations and the word of our pending purchase got out. Just as we were about to close the deal, Peter Finn, the co-CEO of Ruder Finn, called. He had heard that we were in negotiations and said, "I know you're at the altar, but we want to make you an offer." Eventually, we decided to go with Ruder Finn.

When we decided to accept the Ruder Finn offer, I called the first firm and told Tony Esposito, the CFO, and Richard Funess, the President, that we were taking Ruder Finn's offer. I explained our position, thanked them for their interest, expressed my regret about not being able to work with them, and said that I hoped that our paths would cross again. About three years later, Tony called me and said he had just left the firm. Immediately, I arranged for him to meet with Peter Finn and within three days he was hired as Ruder Finn's CFO. Within two weeks, Richard Funess also came over to become Ruder Finn's president. That's the power of networking.

Jill's Story

Ever since I can remember, I dreamed of becoming a public speaker and a media mogul. So, early in my career, I joined the National Speakers Association to learn about speaking and to make contacts. Through NSA, I met Michael Larsen, the literary agent for Jay Conrad Levinson, the bestselling author of the *Guerrilla Marketing* series. Mike and I hit it off. Mike taught want-to-be writers how to get published and I instructed them how to get their books publicized.

After one of our presentations, Mike suggested that I do a book in the Guerrilla series. I just loved the idea! I had wanted to write a book and joining forces with Jay would be ideal. Mike bounced the idea off Jay who approved and we were in business, at least so I thought. However, I soon realized that in order to maintain Promising Promotion, my successful PR business, my burgeoning speaking career, and begin Goodnews Media, I would have to build a support team.

I explained my dilemma to Jay, and he suggested that I call Mark Steisel, a writer friend with whom he had worked. Mark and I met, were on the same wavelength, and he signed on. After we began the project, we realized that the book could benefit from a broader perspective. I called Mike and he suggested that Rick Frishman would make a good complementary partner for me, since I was a woman who ran a boutique West Coast shop and Rick was a man heading a large East Coast agency. What resulted from this networking was the bestselling book *Guerrilla Publicity*.

Through networking I now have an international speaking and writing career. I'm now able to do the things I love, which includes creating Goodnews Media, a company dedicated to inspiring uplifting content, as well as hosting a syndicated radio show called *Do the Dream*. I'm now traveling to the best places, speaking for the best organizations, and spending time with the best people. Because of networking I'm making a fine living, fulfilling my dreams, and totally loving my life!

Generosity Beyond Expectation

When we began this project, we understood that giving was at the core of networking. Everyone told us that to successfully network, you must be willing to give—of your time, your talent, and your advice. It was the central theme of most books and articles. Oh, how they understated it! Over and over again, the people who we interviewed for this book demonstrated that the essence of networking is more than giving, it's generosity: freely giving on an epic scale that exceeds expectations or needs. This book is a testament to generosity. The word "giving" doesn't do justice to the level of help we received; it doesn't even scratch the surface.

Throughout this book we discuss generosity because it is the soul of networking. Generosity is the quality common to all the great networkers we met. They gave instinctively and fully. They were generous in both spirit and deeds. To them, networking meant giving abundantly, often anonymously, without fanfare, but with grace and largesse. With generosity also came warmth, kindness, and genuine delight in providing help. This was the magic!

As a result, the warmth, helpfulness, and generosity that we received far outstripped the rewards we attained from other projects. Besides meeting and getting to know remarkable people—people who we will strive to keep in our lives—we discussed and exchanged views on critical issues. And in the process, it rekindled our occasionally wobbly conviction about the inherent kindness of others.

The best way we know to thank those who have made this book possible is to try to pass the torch. Hopefully, in this book, we can impress upon you that networking is building and being part of a community—a community built on giving generously and inhabited by people who are the best at what they do. Networking is the art of giving to promote the advancement of others. Giving generously triggers the magic we refer to in the title; it ignites a passion that will lift you higher, carry you further, and take you to places that will surpass your wildest dreams.

Action Steps

We have designed this book to provide more than just theoretical explanations of networking. It has been written to teach you about networking, and show you how to systematically build and maintain your own network. It is stuffed with stories and examples that you can follow and adapt to fit your needs.

At the end of a number of the chapters, we have included four action steps that you can follow to identify, practice, and improve your networking skills. When you have completed a chapter, read each action step and give thought to your answers. There are no right or wrong responses. The purpose of the action steps is to awaken your awareness and to help you develop your networking skills.

When answering the action steps, take your time. Complete one set of action steps per week or proceed at your own pace. Addressing the action steps will reinforce major lessons contained in each chapter and help you customize your network to reflect your unique needs and desires.

Happy networking. Thanks for your interest and enjoy this book!

One

Creating Magic

THIS CHAPTER WILL COVER:

What networking is

Connections

Diversity

Reciprocity

Manipulation

Giving from the heart

Fate, coincidence, and luck

"A network is an organized collection
of your personal contacts and your
personal contacts' own contacts."

—Harvey Mackay, author of
Dig Your Well Before You're Thirsty

The night that Sara and Mark moved into their new home, Patsy and Jay dropped by with containers of takeout food, plastic utensils, a bottle of wine, plastic cups, and a large manila folder. They placed the food and drinks on a makeshift table that they fashioned from several unopened cartons, convinced the newcomers to take a well-earned break from unpacking, and they all sat down to an inaugural meal.

After polishing off dessert, Jay handed the new homeowners the manila folder, which contained a computer disk, four refrigerator magnets, and a long list. The list, which Patsy designed, was attractive enough to be displayed on the fridge and the disk could be downloaded to Mark and Sara's computers and synched to their Palm Pilots. Both the print and electronic versions were laid out in four easy-to-read columns and set forth the categories of names, phone numbers, and brief comments about Patsy and Jay's favorite resources. They included the names of restaurants for breakfast, lunch, dinner, and takeout; doctors; pharmacy; dentist; veterinarian; market; hardware store; toy store; jeweler; boutiques; photograph developer; nursery; dry cleaner; tailor; shoemaker; plumber; electrician; gardener; computer repairer; handyman; appliance repairer; beautician; barber; babysitters; and so forth.

Here's an example of what such a list looks like:

Newcomer Reference List

Emergencies (Police, Fire, and Ambulance)	911	
Police (nonemergencies)	555-1212	
St. Vincent's Hospital	555-1730	

Services

Accounting	Marlena Weinstein	555-1040	Works wonders, most accommodating
Alterations	Stitches	555-7755	Fast and reliable, but a bit costly
Appliance repair	Whiz Kids	555-9300	Fixes anything in the home, reasonable
Auto repair	Northgate Auto	555-0046	Good work, foreign and domestic, expensive
Baby-sitting	Maggie Lloyd	555-3365	Kids love her, but needs lots of notice
Cable TV	Gougers	555-9919	
Computer repair	Fearless Computing	555-7893	Will drop everything in an emergency
Dentist	Alissa Yabara	555-9753	Painless, light touch
Doctor	Lawrence Sklar	555-3000	Great bedside manner, really cares
Dry cleaning	Maxibright Cleaners	555-6060	Good and fast, but rough on shirt buttons
Electrician	Alvin Shock	555-4121	Excellent work, but in great demand
Gardener	Green Brothers	555-3131	Reliable, but need direction; explain what you want
Home repairs	Manelli Construction	555-7658	Busy, hard to book, but does great work
Housecleaner	Maria Trujillo	555-0981	Thorough, reliable, and absolutely trustworthy
Lawyer	Peter P. Frunzi Jr.	555-4654	Quick to return calls and is sharp
Limo service	Midnight Blue	555-5171	The best we've ever used
Phone company	AT&T	555-3333	

Services

Plumber	Mackey Stickney	555-9922	Gets to you quickly, does a good job, cleans up
Realtor	Lon Murphy & Co.	555-9898	Knows his stuff, fun to deal with
Taxi service	Speedy's Cabs	555-1111	OK, but could use newer cabs
Tree service	Alex's Tree Service	555-8490	Reasonable and leaves everything neat and trim
Yard work/hauling	Hall and Hall	555-2136	Excellent for getting rid of all sorts of junk

Food

Breakfast	Willie's Café	555-5511	Best eggs in town!
Lunch	Comforts	555-2300	Great salads, light dishes with oriental flavor
Dinner	Thai House	555-7070	Delicious and inexpensive, great takeout
	Enrico's Ristorante	555-3343	You will think you're in Roma, fabulous oysters
	Joe's Taco Lounge	555-2233	Good, quick, and inexpensive; try the Lava Soda
	American Pie	555-1919	First-rate burgers and amazing ribs
Major occasions	Chez Mirabelle	555-3331	Très expensive, but perfect for special evenings
Café	Café de Stijl	555-3737	Great scene, lots of celebs, and terrific, light food
Takeout	Hot Stuff	555-9876	Always call ahead, the lines are endless
Pizza	Vincent's Pizzeria	555-1492	Delicious thin crust, but they don't deliver
Market	Perfect Foods	555-2527	Fabulous produce and fish, buy staples elsewhere
Bakery	Savory	555-1909	Heavenly cookies, can't miss with cakes and pies

Immediately, upon receipt of this gift, the magic began: Sara and Mark were no longer strangers all alone in a new place.

Suddenly, they had contacts and connections—a local network that helped them feel at home in their new house. Now they were armed with a list of top local resources that would have taken them years to gather on their own.

Since Patsy and Jay were sticklers for the best, Sara and Mark knew that they didn't have to research to find resources and verify their qualifications. They could simply refer to the list and be assured that they could find competent, if not always excellent, help. And, better still, when they contacted those on the list and mentioned that they were referred by Patsy and Jay, they received preferential treatment.

What Is Networking?

Networking is the process of building and maintaining relationships. It's the development of a team that will support your efforts and the efforts of your network teammates to reach your respective goals. In practice, networking is the establishment of multiple informal, loosely knit, mutual-support alliances. The object is to build the best possible team.

Networking is about forging bonds and sharing. It's connecting with people who have common interests and objectives and generously give to one another. Networking extends into every aspect of your life; it's something you've been doing all of your life without realizing it. When you recommend a movie, a housecleaner, or a personal trainer, you're networking.

We network as soon as we start making our own decisions. As kids, our friends introduce us to the latest and greatest; they turn us on to a constant flow of new friends and information. Rick's seventeen-year-old daughter, Rachel, said she and her friends use networking with "basically everything we do." Rachel was recommended for her job, found an SAT tutor, met guys whom she dated, and even arranged vacation plans through networking.

The object of networking should not be simply to make

contacts; it should be to make the best possible contacts! Naturally, what constitutes "the best" is subjective and will vary with the individuals and the circumstances involved. However, seeking the best should always be your objective! Pursuing the best will enable you to grow, succeed, and broaden your horizons. It will ensure that you can draw upon the most expert, authoritative input when you need it. It will move you into areas that will challenge, excite, and bring out the best in you.

Goodwill is the foundation for making great contacts; it supports and underlies all of your networking efforts. To successfully network with the best you must constantly create goodwill and then build upon that goodwill to forge bonds that develop into close, meaningful relationships. Networking applies to all areas of life including:

- Friendships
- Romance
- Finances
- Career
- Personal development
- Health and fitness
- Physical environment
- Recreation
- Hobbies and interests

Implicit in networking is the understanding that there will be a giving back, an exchange, "if you do for me, I'll do for you." This unspoken swap of mutual promises underlies networks and keeps them together. Ironically, however, the best networkers are those who give to others because they sincerely love to give and not because they hope to receive something in return. But that doesn't mean that you don't have to give; even the most giving and generous networkers will eventually stop giving when they repeatedly receive nothing in return.

Networks are not built overnight. They take time, patience,

A Fulfilling Way of Life

Networking is a microcosm of life. It's more about how you live your life than what you receive. It's about developing expertise, giving, sharing, and building the best relationships. It's the realization that people and generosity are the most important things in life, that nothing else comes close, and it's about making a dedicated and concerted effort to steer your life in that direction. It's about surrounding yourself with the best in order to build and enjoy a fulfilling life.

and nurturing, especially when you want to network with the best. Initially it may take a bit more time to identify the best, to contact them, cultivate them, and build relationships—but it will be worth it! It will also take time to discover what your network partners need and to continually try to find opportunities to fully satisfy those needs.

Networking Is Not . . .

"Networking isn't sales and sales isn't networking. They're inter-related, but they're not the same," bestselling networking author Susan RoAne advises. "It's a lifestyle, not a work style. The best networkers don't know that they're networking because for them it's a way of life." Top networkers repeatedly stress that they don't network for the financial rewards; rather they network because they love helping people and playing matchmaker.

Networking is a marketing tool, an extremely valuable marketing tool that successful people rely upon heavily. However, if you want long-term success, understand that networking requires a sincere desire to help others. You may be personable, you may be clever, you may have exceptional matchmaking skill, but if you're only in it for the money, or for yourself, ultimately it won't work. Sure, you might be successful for a while, you might even have a good run, but over the long run, people will catch on and the roof will collapse. So instead of concentrating on increasing your profits, put your efforts into helping others. If you do, the sales will follow, as will some other pleasant surprises.

That said, part of the networking magic is the way that it creates converts: Individuals who started networking for purely selfish, self-serving reasons often become addicted to performing selfless acts. Although they began networking in order to boost their careers or to further some personal agenda, they're often surprised to find that building relationships, forging friendships, making connections, and helping others is infinitely more satisfying. They learn to understand that life is a process and start to place a higher premium on how they live rather than on what they receive.

Networking is not just about you; it's about the group, the network, the collective. It's not about pestering people, manipulating, or using them. It's not keeping score, it's not a tit-for-tat or an equal relationship. Networking values effort, it prizes sincere attempts even when they don't achieve what everyone sought.

Transactional Networking

"Sadly, most of us practice transactional networking and we only interact with those who we think we have to in order to complete the transaction," networking coach Sarah Michel observes. "We engage our network only when we need to make a sale, find a job or get a lead. As soon as we get what we want, we drop those people off our radar screens and don't talk to them until we need to make another transaction. We become 'network users' or engage in, as I like to call it, 'network drive-bys.'"

Rules of the Road

Like most disciplines, networking has basic fundamentals that must be fully understood before proceeding further. Although these elements may seem self-evident, think about them and don't take them lightly, because they form the building blocks upon which successful networks must be built. Examine how each of these basic rules applies to you, your methods, and experiences. Identify how others use them to successfully network and ask yourself if their approaches would work for you. Note all of the areas in which you may be deficient and list steps you can take for improvement.

In this chapter, we will introduce you to the basics of networking. At this time, we only wish to plant seeds and lay the groundwork for material that will be subsequently expanded upon in this book. The information being provided is intended to stimulate your thoughts and prepare you for discussions in upcoming chapters.

Relationships

Networking is the art of making connections that blossom into strong, mutually beneficial relationships. Jill is convinced that the magic kicks in when you take it one step further and build relationships with the most outstanding people. "Seeking the best will change your life," she states. "It will expand it, fill it with excitement, surprises, understanding, success, and constant growth. It will lift it beyond the limits that you may not even know you set and make everything brighter, more interesting, and more delicious."

What constitutes "the best" is relative; it depends on who you are and where you are. Your objective should be to always shoot for the best within your reach. And when you form relationships with them, don't stop there! Keep moving—move into bigger arenas, bigger ponds where you land bigger and better fish. Make it your crusade to continually meet the most outstanding people.

Pursuing relationships with the best can be intimidating. The top people are often daunting, hard to reach, and dismissive. Usually, they have pressing demands on their time and when—and if—you reach them, they can be brusque, distant, and unresponsive. On the other hand, many at the top thirst for new ideas, approaches, and experiences. They are consumed with their areas of expertise and want to deal with the best, those who are on their plane, with whom they can truly communicate, share, and explore. If you demonstrate that you belong, they will eagerly welcome you.

Relationships hinge on the quality of the connections that are forged. When connections are weak or matches are incompatible, productive networking relationships cannot be built. However, when connections bond, strong relationships can emerge. Bonding and sharing make relationships work.

If you want excellence, you must turn to those who do things excellently: people you can count on, learn from, and whose work you don't have to redo. Working with those who are excellent raises the bar; it improves the results you have the right to expect and the level of projects in which you can participate. It places you—and the work you perform and receive—on a higher plateau, a stratum inhabited by the best. When you're dealing on those lofty levels, the rewards are also higher.

Building relationships with the best is the networker's primary objective. Short-term goals such as finding a job, a babysitter, or a good sushi bar are secondary goals. Forging strong relationships should be your top priority because they last long after the job, the sitter, or the hamachi is gone. And network relationships can continually help you find better jobs, more reliable sitters, and fresher, more delicious fish.

Quest for the Best

Legendary chef Alice Waters, founder of the four-star restaurant Chez Panisse in Berkeley, California, is an acknowledged international culinary authority. Unquestionably, she is at the top of her field. Waters has trained, worked with, and developed close ties to many of the world's great chefs. As a result, her "Paris list" has become the bible for her network members who travel to Paris and want the best. Waters's list includes not only her favorite eateries, places most of us would never discover, but also her tips about shops, markets, and other mouth-watering attractions. Her list has been built on the recommendations Waters has received from her network, which is made up of many of the world's most acclaimed chefs, restaurateurs, food critics, teachers, writers, and gourmets. Because of her stature in culinary circles and the extraordinary quality of her network, Waters' list is a sought-after treasure.

Diversity

In building a network, create a multifaceted superstructure that includes contacts who possess a wide variety of skills, interests, and backgrounds. Fill your life with outstanding network members whose help can quickly be accessed so that their expertise will be available to you when you need it.

Make your network diverse. Fill it with top experts in areas that differ from and complement your skills. Think of the members of your network as your support team; consider them experts who are fluent in languages you don't speak. Blend a mix of talents, interests, age, gender, race, and backgrounds. Besides filling in your gaps, the differences can stimulate, enrich, and expose you to knowledge and perspectives that can broaden your life.

Spreading Your Blanket

When you visualize your network, don't picture it as a chain or a single column of contacts who all share similar areas of expertise. Instead, see it as a multidimensional mesh-work made up of people with differing talents, experiences, and viewpoints that radiate and link in all directions. Ideally, your network will spread in many directions so it can operate like a blanket to cover any conceivable topic, discipline, or target.

By not diversifying your network, you run the risk of having a group with too many similar skills and areas of glaring weaknesses. You also run the danger of duplicating yourself, of surrounding yourself with "yes" men and women, which undermines a major asset of networks—an influx of fresh, independent support.

Although it's essential to surround yourself with the best network members that you can reach, be careful not to consider anyone too small or insignificant for membership in your network. There is always a role they can play and you never know what connections people have or what the future may bring. The receptionist who greeted you today might be the executive assigned to your account tomorrow; the mechanic who services your car may work on the CEO's racing team and hang out with him or her at the track; and the kid who delivered your lunch just might be the son of the company's founder.

Jill believes that *everyone* she meets may:

- Need her services
- Know of someone who needs her services or provides services that Jill herself might need
- Offer something that someone else she knows might need

Reciprocity

In life, we all try to get things from each other; that's how the world works and has always worked. From ancient times, we have been a people who belonged to tribes and clannish groups. We built societies in which we lived, worked, and raised families together. In these societies, each member had specific roles that he or she performed for the benefit of the group. We gave to and helped each other. And, we also received.

Networks operate on similar principles. When it comes to networking, an implied promise exists that, "If you help me, I'll help you." This implied promise is the bond upon which networks and societies are built. Without the assurance of reciprocal help, many network members would not give. In networking, reciprocating, returning favors, and giving back is not merely expected, it's demanded; it's the price you pay to be a network member.

Network members are realists. They understand that most requests have more than one motive. They know that the reason given may not be all there is. They also know all too well that many good-intentioned individuals don't or can't follow through and deliver what they promised. Realists accept the fact that folks get busy, face other demands, and simply forget. What they won't abide, however, is repeated, out-and-out exploitation by those whom they have helped because networking involves giving and taking, not exploiting.

Remember the following four rules of successful, reciprocal networking:

1. You can't always be the connectee; you must also be the connector.
2. You can't always be the taker; you must also give.
3. To build a successful network you must be prepared to give at least two or three items for every one you receive.
4. Better yet, don't count; just give!

Give generously; don't skimp. If you expect to receive more than you give, you'll be bitterly disappointed. Sure, you may get away with being a skinflint once, twice, or even several times, but sooner or later people will catch on, feel abused, and avoid you. And if you get anything, it will be drastically less than you gave and probably more than you deserve.

If you want to build relationships with the best, go the extra mile. Extend yourself, be lavish, and make grand gestures to impress upon your contact how far you're willing to go to cement the relationship. To attract the best, give the best and give your best.

Train yourself to spot leads or opportunities for your network partners. To identify leads for partners requires you to understand their needs and how these needs can be best filled. Think of networks as friendships. Your connection to network members is a bond built on the same basic principles as friendship. They are:

- Helping
- Sharing
- Trusting

Both networks and friendships are intended to be long-lasting and enduring, not just fleeting or hit-and-run contacts. A network, like a friendship, will work only if you're asking, "What can I do for you?" It will not work if you're only asking, "What can I get from you?"

Savvy players understand that networking fields are seldom level. The rich, powerful, and famous are usually better connected and endowed. They have more clout than others, especially newcomers who are just starting out. So, most beginner networkers must try harder, be more accommodating, more assertive, give more, and seize every initiative, especially when they're trying to connect with people at the top.

Direct your efforts and give your contacts something they

Renewable Resources

"In a competitive environment, when we use and exploit each other and take everything we possibly can from network resources, we create a nonsustainable resource that collapses on itself because people feel used," Bernhard Dohrmann, cofounder of IBI Global, Inc., explains. "In a cooperative network, you reward everyone who helps you appropriately for the degree and level of the help received. Sometimes, it's a 'thank you' or a gift and sometimes it's stock, fees or money. There should always be a reward for a contact that made a benefit to you. If you have a benefit, you should give a reward of one kind or another including recognition. Those are sustainable networks that will not collapse on themselves, they will always supernetwork and expand during your lifetime."

really want or need; anything less may be ignored or sloughed off. Jump the gun; instead of waiting for that powerhouse you've been courting to ask for a favor, find great resources that he or she could use and hook him or her up. To be a good network partner, you must help, help, help. And when you're tired, help some more!

Manipulation

Although networkers understand that everyone wants something, they resent being manipulated, used, or conned. If, in the list of offenses, forgetting or being too busy to reciprocate is shoplifting, then out-and-out manipulation is first-degree murder and often carries a life sentence.

If network members feel used, if they believe that you're only out for yourself, they won't take your calls and they certainly won't help you. Worse yet, they'll tell others about your deceit and once the word gets out, you'll find yourself alone with nowhere to turn.

Networking requires a delicate balance. People who can help you can just as easily harm you if you don't deal with them wisely. If they feel that the only reason you contact them is for what you can get, you'll probably lose a friend, a good contact, and, maybe, your reputation. Even the most altruistic and dedicated networkers won't continue to help those who won't give back.

Think about your own experiences. We've all had "friends" who called only when they needed something. Remember what it was like when, after not hearing from him or her for the longest time, then all of a sudden the phone rings and you're being treated like his or her closest friend. These people are users, manipulators, takers. Hopefully, you've gotten them out of your life by now.

Remember how it felt after you delivered, when the phone calls stopped and your user friend vanished. Didn't you feel used, ripped off, and abused? Would you have volunteered to help that person again and subject yourself to further pain?

Networks operate in a similar fashion. Just as you distanced yourself from your user friend, network members—even the most generous of them—will dump those who won't give back. It's basic self-preservation. So if you want to network, it *must* be reciprocal.

Passion

The most successful networkers build relationships with others because they love people and the dynamics of relation-ships, and are irrepressible matchmakers. They love sharing their lives and experiences and being closely involved with others. It gives them a sense of community and purpose. They are the ones who are always trying to fix single people up on dates, send friends to their favorite hideaway resort, or introduce them to a cool new acquaintance. The top connectors are "people" people who come from the heart; for them, matchmaking is a passion.

Scores of successful networkers have told us that they derive more joy from building relationships than they do from the ultimate results. They proudly proclaim that they're "networkers" and derive great pleasure from their work. They love nothing more than meeting new people, getting to know them, and then connecting them with others.

Networking is built on enthusiasm and passion, which savvy networkers don't fake. Most people can immediately spot fakers, which turns them off and scares them away—and that makes it awfully hard to network.

Most successful networkers usually love:

- People
- What they do
- Giving of themselves without restriction

Networkers such as these openly refer those they trust to their resources. To them, matchmaking is a game, an opportunity, a calling. They feel that the more solid relationships they help create, the more successful THEY are. Instead of avoiding opportunities to play matchmaker, they jump at them. In response to requests for the names of contacts, the best networkers immediately reel off a few names and then repeatedly inject, "Oh, and also take down the name of _____ _____" and, "Oh yeah, _____ _____" and "Then don't forget ____ _____."

Generosity usually pays off because network members will rush to help those who have aided them or members of their network. It's the networker's way of saying "thanks," passing the baton, and playing the network game at its highest level. Your generosity will be appreciated by the top people; those who

Quest for the Best

Rick spent a day with Arnold Palmer when the golf immortal was the number-one sports celebrity in the world. Rick was indelibly impressed by how warm, respectful, and accessible Palmer was to all his fans and to the media. Arnold Palmer is known as the "king" because he always took time to pose for pictures and sign autographs. In fact, he told Rick that it was an "honor," because it was his fans who made him a success and that he owed everything to them.

don't appreciate it are usually not worthy of being your network partners.

In most cases, it doesn't pay to hide your true agenda. It's usually best to be open and clearly explain exactly what you want. For example, "Can you introduce me to Jack Jones?" If you sense reluctance or misgivings, back off. Everyone has personal limits so don't push or you may turn a potentially good source into someone who avoids you.

When your contact is forthcoming, always express your appreciation and ask how you can reciprocate. Some contacts will be direct and tell you exactly what they expect while others will be silent or noncommittal. If a contact wants a referral fee, clarify in advance how much he or she expects to avoid problems down the road. If he or she is too demanding, express your feelings up front or it will come back to haunt you at a later date.

Trust

Trust is an essential ingredient for successful networks. For networks to succeed, mutual trust is a must! Top networkers will not recommend or extend themselves for those who do not consistently deliver the best; anything less will tarnish their reputations and limit their potential returns. Each member of your network must be completely confident that they can always rely upon you for:

Excellent service. The products or services you provide must be excellent; good or adequate will not be enough. If you hope to network with the best, whatever you provide must shine. It must be memorable and distinguish you from the crowd. The best only want to deal with the best, so network contacts will be drawn to you because of the high quality of your work. However, if the level of what you deliver falls short, they'll quickly drop you and turn to the next pretty smile. People take pride in dealing with the best. They want the best doctor, piano teacher, or house painter, and are usually willing to pay for them. Providing excellence distinguishes you and anything less will quickly send you back with the rest of the pack, where it's easy to get buried and forgotten.

Honesty. Network contacts must:

- Know that you will always deliver what you promise. They don't want excuses, they want, and *deserve*, results.
- Be certain that you will give them honest feedback, especially when it may hurt or be awkward.
- Unequivocally believe that you will honor your relationships and not disclose or misuse their confidential information or try to undermine their efforts.
- Be sure that you will not misrepresent or abuse your relationship. If it turns out that you can't deliver what you thought you could, then inform those who are depending on you so that they can minimize the damage.

High standards. A problem that is rampant in networking is that network members recommend too many people who are not top-notch. Often, they lack the standards to know excellence or their recommendation may be to return a favor or make you feel that they are helping you. Other networks spread themselves too thin and try to provide everything to everyone. To build a reputation for trust:

- Recommend only the best people for each particular job.
- When you're aware of problems with otherwise excellent performers, inform network members regarding their flaws. For example, "John does fabulous work, but he's slow and his projects are invariably late." Being fully informed helps network members make their own decisions, gets you off the hook, and enhances your trust quotient.

Good fits. Networking is matchmaking, and certain pairings will never create a harmonious fit. We all have unique qualities, values, methods, personalities, styles, and objectives, which may not be compatible with those with whom we are matched. The best way to make consistently good matches is to know the people involved, their assets and liabilities, and try to anticipate problems that might arise. Find out the parties' likes, dislikes, and basic requirements and when in doubt, ask. Put it straight to

---

Qualities That Create Lack of Trust

- Not keeping your word
- Not showing up
- Not giving credit
- Routinely being late
- Exaggerating
- Boasting and bragging
- Not calling when you promised
- Always putting yourself first
- Taking more than your share
- Bashing competitors
- Not admitting your mistakes
- Blaming others

them: "What do you want?" And, continue questioning them until you feel you understand precisely what they want.

Always deliver what you promise because it reinforces people's trust in you. People buy from and want to be associated with people they trust. They don't like to buy from those who they think are trying to sell them, which is why so many hate the experience of buying a car. Networks are built on trust and cannot last without mutual trust.

Fate, Coincidence, and Luck

We've called this book *Networking Magic* in deference to the fact that networking often produces baffling and mysterious outcomes. Networking can put us together with people who can send us soaring to heights that we might never have scaled by ourselves, and launch us off in directions that we could never have imagined. The title of this book also conjures up the frequent intervention of events that we can't control, but which we can prepare for, recognize, and capitalize on when they occur.

When networking, expect the unexpected. No one knows how things will develop or where they will land. The best-laid plans, the most detailed preparation may fail; the most heartfelt, well-intentioned promises may not be fulfilled. Life, serendipity, the universe—call it what you will—has an amazing way of changing the most well-thought-out plans. When this occurs, and you can be sure that it will, trust your instincts and, when necessary, adjust your focus. When the unexpected strikes, it may be time to move in new directions.

Put your faith in people; ask for their help because they love to help. They love a good story, they love happy endings, and, when given the chance, will do more than their part to create that perfect ending. When you ask for help, most people are flattered. They feel closer to you and believe that they have an investment in your success. When you network with the best,

Quest for the Best

In 1982, Stanton Royce was a single father of children aged eight and three living in a small Ohio Valley steel town. He wanted to find a wife, but realized that his local options were limited. So he created a public relations campaign that he hoped would attract national media attention to his quest for a wife. He invested his meager budget in advertisements in two local newspapers, a billboard, and a local radio show that reached West Virginia and Pennsylvania. Sure enough, the local media picked up Royce's story and he received extensive coverage.

A woman in Pennsylvania saw Royce on a Wheeling, West Virginia, news broadcast and contacted a friend abroad. Her friend told her coworker about Royce, who told her sister, who introduced him to the woman who became his wife. Royce and his wife, who is a physician and "an incredible person," have now been happily married for over nineteen years.

they have a greater incentive to help you because providing you with anything but the best could tarnish their reputation.

Put yourself out there. Give people the chance to help because that's when the magic happens. Wonderful, marvelous, greater than expected bonuses occur when you let your friends in, when you let the world in, and when you let the world work its magic. Position yourself to experience the magic. Inform your friends and network partners about your needs and allow them to help.

The Right Attitude

To open yourself up to successful networking, you may have to change some of your attitudes and work to do the following:

- *Be optimistic.* See everything as an opportunity or a step that could lead to a break. See everyone as a potential ally, a network partner with whom you can provide mutual help.
- *Remain flexible.* No matter how committed or involved you are to a specific strategy, method, or approach, be open to its failure and have some backup plans. Like good door-to-door salespeople, carry a number of products in your sample case.
- *Have alternatives.* Realize that other options might be more realistic or productive.
- *Be alert.* Don't simply lose yourself so deeply in your endeavors that you can't recognize the warning signs. Pay attention to those you speak with and learn to recognize danger signs.
- *Monitor developments.* Constantly monitor your situation and make necessary adjustments when appropriate.
- *Be grateful and express it.* Appreciate the efforts of others and make sure to tell them how thankful you are. Actively look for ways to express your appreciation.
- *Shoot for the best.* Always try to find who is the best and then create a plan to reach him or her. If your top target is out of your reach, identify alternatives, but still try to reach the top.

Fate, coincidence, and luck can also hand you gifts, unexpected bounties, manna from above. Develop your skills, increase your expertise, and frequent places filled with rainmakers. Place yourself in places and situations where you can demonstrate your talents in the best light to help those miracles along. Keep learning; remain active, involved, and productive. If you simply sit around and expect to be discovered, bring plenty of reading material because you may have an awfully long, lonely wait.

A Way of Life

Networking is more than just a marketing tool; it's a way of life. It's about how you lead your life, not just about closing a deal. Although innumerable businesses have been built through networking, the principles involved are basic. Networking is the building and maintaining of relationships and relationships require caring, helping, kindness, decency, trust, and honoring others. In a nutshell, networking is about giving and giving generously and constantly striving for the best.

The top networkers understand that people and their relationships with them are the centerpieces and the most important assets in their lives. That's why they've built their lives around increasing and maintaining these assets and have wide circles of loyal supporters in their lives.

Quest for the Best

"Hollywood and the motion picture business are all about networking," according to film producer Jesse B'Franklin. "Almost everything in the industry depends on networking. When I first got to LA, I was out four or five nights each week to screenings, parties, book fairs, film festivals, whatever. I needed to meet people, to make contacts and get my name known. Here, people don't ask, 'How are you?' They ask, 'What are you doing?' When my friends get asked out, they never know whether guys are asking for romantic reasons or for business reasons.

"You can be sitting in the dentist chair, shot up with Novocaine, your mouth stuffed with cotton and the dentist will pitch you for a script he wrote," B'Franklin says. Her husband, director Carl Franklin, decided to cast Don Cheadle in *Devil in a Blue Dress* after they ran into each other and sat interminably in a doctor's waiting room.

Action Steps

Here are some exercises to do as a start in finding ways to make networking a part of your life.

1. Set forth three steps that will make you a better connector.

_____

_____

_____

2. Identify the four best people who you could enlist to add diversity to your network regardless of whether or not you can reach them.

_____

_____

_____

3. List three ways that you can reciprocate for the help others give you.

_____

_____

_____

4. Name three changes you can make to improve your attitude in order to network more successfully.

_____

_____

_____

Two

The Boardroom Dinners

THIS CHAPTER WILL COVER:

Boardroom's background

The logistics

The guests

The dinners

The discussions

Hosting your own
networking dinners

"All men are caught in an inescapable
network of mutuality, tied in a single
garment of destiny. Whatever affects
one directly, affects all indirectly."

—Rev. Martin Luther King Jr.

Boardroom, Inc., is a publisher of books and newsletters located in Stamford, Connecticut. It was founded in 1971 by Marty Edelston and is best known for publishing the newsletters: *Bottom Line/Personal, Bottom Line/Health, Bottom Line/Tax Hotline,* and *Bottom Line/Tomorrow.* Boardroom hosts monthly dinners that are so inspirational and provide such unparalleled networking opportunities that we decided to devote a complete chapter to them.

According to those who have attended, Boardroom dinners exemplify the best. They are the best, most stimulating, and entertaining networking events. They are attended by the best, most interesting, and articulate experts. They are held in one of the world's best and most beautiful restaurants, which serves world-class food. The Boardroom dinners also present an exceptional, easy-to-adapt model that you can tailor and use to substantially boost the quality of your networking and your life.

The Boardroom formula is to surround yourself with remarkable people—the most brilliant, exceptional, and accomplished individuals you can find—and to create an atmosphere that will encourage them to share their wealth of ideas, wisdom, and experiences. It sounds basic and, in some ways, it is. However, Boardroom has perfected the execution of this idea and

Success Knowledge

"The dinners are incredible," public speaker and marketing consultant Ken Glickman says of the Boardroom dinners. "Marty brings together such truly amazing people. He creates an atmosphere that encourages people to talk about what they know and the exciting things that are occurring in their area. These evenings create a tremendous amount of enthusiasm and positive energy and besides learning a lot and making great contacts, I always leave with enormous motivation to make something exciting happen. You learn *success knowledge*, which is the knowledge of how things really work, and the only people who can teach you that are the people who have made things happen. Marty fills the room with those types of people."

elevated it to glittering heights that excite the imagination as well as the guests. The result is networking and human interaction at its very best—dazzling, stimulating, and inspiring experiences that can entertain, teach, uplift, and help build exceptional relationships.

As you read about the Boardroom dinners, think how you can host equivalent events on a scale that will fit your budget, needs, and your particular circumstances.

The Background

Boardroom's publications rely heavily on articles and information submitted by the foremost experts and authorities in their fields. This approach is an outgrowth of Edelston's curiosity and his lifelong passion to acquire knowledge and understanding.

A voracious reader, Edelston was frequently inspired by the books he read, and so he often hired the authors to write articles for Boardroom publications on subjects that fascinated him. He also made a concerted effort to meet and build relationships with the authors of "the best books" and probe their expertise more deeply.

The idea for the Boardroom dinners came to Edelston after he attended some stimulating lunches and dinners hosted by friends and business contacts. He found the guests and the conversations so magical that he decided to try to recapture the experiences by hosting similar events. While compiling the names of potential guests to invite to his dinners, Edelston realized that the experts who contributed to his publications and his existing contacts constituted a fabulous list. So he invited them to his dinners. Since then, he has continued to supplement his list with other experts he meets, hears of, or with whom he works.

Originally, Edelston held his dinners in his New York City office, but then he rented an apartment solely to house those events. He hired a great caterer and sent out invitations. Experts attended, met other experts, engaged each other in riveting discussions, and enjoyed exciting, enlightening evenings. And no one enjoyed them more than Edelston. Soon, guests told friends about the wonders of Edelston's dinners and as the word got out, the dinners became coveted events and destinations.

Eventually, Edelston's gatherings evolved into the monthly Boardroom dinners that have been held in a private dining room at New York City's renowned Four Seasons restaurant since 1994. The Boardroom dinners are a tribute to Edelston's deep curiosity, his thirst for knowledge, and his unyielding passion to build relationships with the best and the brightest. They also demonstrate his joy and generosity in sharing with others.

Rick, who has attended Boardroom dinners, considers them a tribute to Marty. "Everyone is there because of Marty. The dinners center around Marty and reflect his interests, his questions and his standards. Marty's dinners are networking events that pay homage to a master networker and to his amazing passion for the best. They have become so famous because you get to spend time with remarkable people who you normally would never get the opportunity to even meet. It is an honor to be invited."

The Logistics

Boardroom dinners are cohosted by Edelston and Brian Kurtz, Boardroom's Executive Vice President. The number of guests usually ranges between twelve and twenty-seven, but eighty people signed up for one recent Boardroom dinner. Kurtz believes that groups of sixteen to twenty-two are ideal because seating larger groups is more difficult and tends to make the evenings less intimate. With groups up to twenty-two, ten guests can be seated at both sides of a single, long table with Kurtz and Edelston at either end.

Guests are selected from a database that Boardroom maintains and includes authors who have written articles for Boardroom or individuals who were featured in or interviewed for articles in the company's publications. Other invitees are experts Edelston and Kurtz have met at conferences, meetings, or other events and authorities who have worked for or consulted with Boardroom. In addition, guests might have little or no connection with Boardroom other than the hosts' interest in them and their expertise. Selection is geared toward inviting the best people, not toward achieving particular mixes or adhering to any set rules.

Dinners are planned one year in advance and a schedule of the upcoming dinners for the year is sent to those on the invitation database. Out-of-town guests can then plan to attend a dinner during a time when they will be visiting New York or they can arrange trips to coincide with the date of a specific dinner. Each guest sends back a reply card, which is enclosed with the schedule, to inform Boardroom of the dinner he or she wishes to attend. Boardroom keeps a list of all responses and as each dinner approaches, confirms the date with each scheduled guest.

An invitation to Boardroom dinners is a hot and prestigious ticket. Besides being invited to dine at one of the world's great restaurants, guests are given the rare opportunity to spend an evening engaged in stimulating conversations with an amazing collection of fascinating experts. Simply being considered as a guest is exceptionally flattering.

Prior to each dinner, Edelston and Kurtz review the guests' biographies and create the seating arrangement. Edelston and Kurtz consider the seating arrangement crucial and strive to make good matches. They strategically seat guests to build upon obvious synergies, which they hope will encourage lively exchanges and the creation of stimulating relationships.

The Guests

Guests decide which dinner they wish to attend, so the mix is random and varies from dinner to dinner. Kurtz believes that the randomness and constant changes make the dinners more dynamic. Usually, the guests represent a broad assortment of disciplines, but it can vary. "At one dinner we had six doctors with various specialties, at another we had seven people who were in direct marketing and at yet another, nobody was in health care, but six financial analysts attended," Kurtz said. "We could plan it if we wanted to, but by not planning it we end up with something more interesting."

Since Boardroom places a higher premium on the quality of the guests than on the areas of their expertise, a diverse range of businesses, professions, and disciplines have gathered around the table over the years. Guests have been spellbound by information disclosed by experts on everything from terrorism to sex therapy. Medical researchers have explained the latest breakthroughs in their fields and a former White House staffer from the Kennedy White House has shared inside stories about the JFK era.

The Dinners

Each dinner is preceded by a cocktail hour, at which time guests arrive, meet one another, and mingle. Guests then move to a private dinning room where place cards instruct them where to sit. When the guests are seated, Edelston and/or Kurtz welcome them. Since some guests have attended past dinners, they know why they were invited, but others have no idea. So the hosts explain that the purpose of the dinners is to bring together some of the brightest and most interesting people who can be assembled in one room during one evening and to encourage them to share ideas and information while they enjoy a fabulous meal. "Things that you can ordinarily do on a weeknight, like going to the movies or the theater are okay, but there's nothing like the stimulation you get spending time with brilliant people," Edelston stresses.

The hosts then go around the room to introduce each guest to the group, informing them about his or her area of expertise. In his introductions, Kurtz finds himself constantly saying that this or that guest "is the world's best _____." Can you think of a better way to spend an evening?

When they are introduced, each guest is asked to share something with the group. For example, what they're most proud of, or what they would like to have everybody in the room know about them. Guests may also be asked a probing question such as, "What's new in your field?" or "What are you working on?"

The hosts try to move the introductory phase along briskly because they want to make sure that all of the guests are properly introduced. However, guests can become so engrossed with information that another guest is sharing, or find him or her so interesting, that they ask lots of questions, which slows the pace.

For example, when a terrorism expert spoke about information he learned at the CIA, the other guests immediately peppered him with so many questions that they stopped everything cold. "When you get great people around the table, the conversations and the dynamics are really mind-blowers," Edelston noted. "Fabulous stuff happens."

When the main course is served, the guests have the opportunity to meet, talk, and get to know each other. After the main course, salad is served; Edelston rings a chime to get the guests' attention and to resume the program. Prior to each dinner, Edelston and Kurtz review information about the guests who are expected to attend and they select stimulating topics to kick off discussions. If eminent physicians are to be in attendance, a good opening might be to ask them what is the latest, most groundbreaking medical research nearing completion in their specialty area. The hosts also try to identify which guests might try to monopolize the room and prepare appropriate responses to bring others into the conversations.

The Discussions

The central group discussions begin when one host directs an opening question to an expert. Opening questions are intended to elicit reactions and group participation. Although the expert initially carries the ball, everyone present is encouraged to speak and ask questions. The hosts constantly monitor the discussions to keep them moving and usually let them follow their natural course. However, if a topic plays out or if a guest hogs the floor, a host will step in and change the subject by posing a question to another guest. Over the years, the hosts have become adept at reading guests' reactions, and, since they know the guests' bios, they can smoothly move discussions in new directions. As a result, the group rarely stays on one topic for an entire dinner and the conversations seldom stagnate.

"When you have people sitting around a table talking passionately about their areas of expertise and sharing new developments and insider stories, whether it's psychology, cardiology, pending legislation, entertainment, finances, or sex, it's simply amazing," Kurtz exclaims. "It becomes a phenomenal evening and you end up learning tons of remarkable stuff in addition to making unbelievable network contacts."

At one time, Edelston recorded the dinners to get story ideas for future Boardroom publications. Although the proceedings are no longer recorded, the hosts inform their guests that they may use information discussed during the conversations as inspirations for future content for their publications. In addition, a member of Boardroom's editorial staff usually attends each dinner to take notes so that staff writers can follow up on good story ideas with guest interviews.

Guests are free to exchange business cards, and during the dinner, a list is circulated to get each guest's e-mail address, which will be added to Boardroom's invitation database. After each dinner, Boardroom sends follow-up packages to guests that include samples of its newsletters, one of its new books, and a present such as a Boardroom umbrella. A full listing of the guests' contact information and their specialties are also provided with the packages.

"The people I've met through these dinners are remarkable," Kurtz said. "And co-hosting these dinners has taken me to a new level of intimacy with a lot of our guests. E-mail makes it easy for me to keep in touch with them and I'm always referring people to this one or that one. I've got a great Rolodex and I'm a good networker, but this has expanded my networking well beyond my core competencies.

"When I first started going to the dinners, they made me feel kind of small because I realized how huge the world is and how insignificant each of us is. But now, I've gone completely over in the other direction, which is that the world is such a fantastic place. Everybody is an expert in something and when you can share your expertise and your passions in a way that is totally giving, extraordinary things occur," Kurtz added. That's networking magic!

Hosting Your Own

The moral of the Boardroom story is to surround yourself with remarkable people. You owe it to yourself and those you love to meet and build relationships with the best. Nothing can improve your life like associating with terrific people; it gives your life fullness. And, remember, when you build relationships with extraordinary individuals, you also become privy to their networks, which are usually composed of equally outstanding people.

So shoot for the stars, the top, the highest rung you can reach. However, in the process, don't abandon your present cronies and network partners. Add new faces, new spice, new minds, and new ideas, but also don't forget your tried-and-true contacts.

Take the initiative and put yourself together with those who can stimulate you, excite you, teach you, broaden you, and make the nights fly by. Top people are frequently open to new experiences and new relationships. Some may initially say no to your approaches, but there is always tomorrow and if your dinners or gatherings or whatever you do build good buzz, they'll be clamoring for an invitation. Naturally, we all can't host lavish dinners at the Four Seasons or draw from the same remarkable talent pool as Boardroom. Yet, we all can start small gatherings filled with the most exceptional people we know and then build upon that.

Start with the best people you can reach. Invite your most interesting, enjoyable, entertaining friends and contacts. Invite people you've heard about, but don't know. Invite people whom you've wanted to meet. Select guests who are experts in fields that interest you and in areas that you know nothing about. It doesn't have to be all talk. If you know musicians, poets, or entertainers, then ask them to your gathering to liven up and diversify the mix.

Work on a scale that you can afford. Although good food certainly helps, great people should be your top priority. So when you're starting out, think first about the quality of your guests, about attracting the very best people. And if the food is a way to attract heavy hitters, do whatever you can, within your means, to get them to the table. Then get them talking.

Prepare and ask questions that will make your guests expound. Once they're talking, sit back and let the magic work. Only interject if a guest filibusters, gets too far off course, or the discussion becomes dry. Then steer the conversation gently by asking another question that could ignite more stimulating talk.

Once you get rolling, do it right. Kurtz recommends sparing no expense, "And if that means doing fewer dinners, but making them all 'perfect,' I would recommend that."

Action Steps

1. State three ways you could adapt the Boardroom dinners to work for you.

   _____

   _____

   _____

2. What would you like to accomplish by hosting your events?

   _____

   _____

   _____

3. Identify the five best people you could invite to anchor your events.

_____

_____

_____

4. What new features would you add to your events?

_____

_____

_____

Three

Building the Best Network

THIS CHAPTER WILL COVER:

Focusing

Listening

Taking inventory

Helping

Getting organized

You are your product

Start close to home

Identify hurdles

Promises

"The quickest way to the top is to take everyone with you."

—Bernhard Dohrmann,
cofounder IBI Global, Inc.

If you want to succeed, build a great team composed of the best players, a true all-star team. A great team multiplies your prospects for success by enabling you to form relationships with powerful people who can make your dreams come true. A great network supports your strengths, fills in your weaknesses, and allows you to build on your teammates' accomplishments. When you have a great team, people assume that you too are great, and they will stand in line to get to know you, do business with you, and help you. They will also be delighted to pay your price.

Okay, so you understand the value of a strong network. But how do you get started in building a great network?

Unless you've been living in total seclusion, you already have a network in place. And your network is probably more extensive than you realize. It may not be a great network yet, but it's a beginning and a place from which to build. Your network most likely consists of your family, friends, schoolmates, and business associates. It includes people with whom you've conducted business, socialized, or otherwise interacted. In addition, the members of your network have networks of their own from which you can benefit. For example, if your accountant is a member of your network, so are all the members of your accountant's network.

Quest for the Best

Johnny Carson's job on the *Tonight Show* was the pinnacle for talk show hosts. When Carson was preparing to leave the show, the top candidates to succeed him were Jay Leno and David Letterman. At the time, Leno was regularly performing his comedy act throughout the country. Letterman, on the other hand, remained in the New York City area and concentrated on his own late-night show.

According to industry sources, in every city where Leno performed, he called the top brass at the local NBC affiliate stations and said, "Hi, this is Jay Leno. I'm in town this week. If you would like for me to pop by your studio for an interview or to entertain your staff for a few minutes, just plug me in." He also befriended the station executives and invited them to his shows.

Just before it was time for NBC to decide on the permanent *Tonight Show* host, Leno called his friends at the affiliates and asked them to put in a good word for him with NBC. In turn, the affiliates contacted the network and said, "Go with my friend Jay Leno!" The power of Jay Leno's "network networking" helped him get one of the most coveted and high-profile jobs in television.

To build great networks, you need great people: great lawyers, doctors, dentists, accountants, insurance agents, friends . . . you get the idea. Identify the best people; don't just find out who services computers, discover who the *best* people are who service computers. Learn all you can about them and then work backward to figure out how you can meet them.

To find the best computer service, Rick suggests contacting the best, most successful people you know who rely on computers. "Their livelihood depends on computers, and they need them to make a living. If their computers go down, they need to get them up as soon as possible. They use the best people and can give you the best recommendations," he advised.

Continually expand and upgrade your existing network. Everything always changes and what constitutes a great network today, could be less than great tomorrow. Network members drop out and lose interest: They change businesses, interests, and their lives and so will you. In networking, expanding and upgrading is a never-ending process: Heads of states, CEOs, and established leaders at every strata of society are constantly seeking to find the best people and incorporate them into their networks, to add them to their teams. So the process of expanding and upgrading never stops; it's what building a network is all about.

Focusing on the Best

To expand and upgrade your network requires focus. Once you realize that you have a network, it's time to sharpen your focus and begin to see with new eyes. Continually look for new and better network members.

Focus on the best. Identify and keep lists of the best people in every discipline, even if you are not interested in them or their specialty area. List them merely because they are the best. Ask your friends, family, and associates who they would rate as the best. Write down names that you find in articles, on the Web, or on TV. Ask journalists, reporters, and people in every field. Regularly update your list of the best. Like everything else, the people who actually are the best will change, so make sure you know who the current aces are.

Search for links that tie your network members with the names on your lists. Look toward virtually everyone you meet and everything you experience. Find opportunities to approach your targets and ways that you can help them reach their goals. Follow the example of the successful people in your life. Have you noticed how frequently they take new information and relate it to their particular area of expertise? Have you observed that writers tend to see everything as material for potential stories, financiers always look at the bottom line, publicists think about promotional possibilities, comics turn everything into humor, lawyers probe for hidden liabilities, and medical workers zero in on health?

Successful networkers operate on the same principle. They're obsessed with making the best connections and therefore instinctively search for them. Accomplished networkers see the world in terms of leads, contacts, and opportunities that will bring them closer to network relationships. They view the world optimistically and see every possibility as an opening that could lead them to their pot of gold.

Examine how the successful people you know process new information. Then apply their methods to your situation.

Developing Awareness

Focus starts with awareness. Usually, it's a painless process that is a natural by-product of your interests and it occurs without planning or effort. When you are truly interested or involved, doors open through which you can see. How many times after being introduced to something new, have you found yourself merrily breezing along when suddenly your antennae pick up signals alerting you to information about that subject—a subject in which just a short time ago you had little or no interest. Before long, everything concerning that subject seems compelling and everything seems to relate to it.

The same holds true for networking. In most cases, your contacts have been around for quite a while. However, you confined them to specific niches. To you they were friends, family, business associates, or service people, not potential network contacts or stepping-stones to new connections. When you

Now You See It

Isn't it amazing that as soon as you buy a car, you notice how many identical models are on the road? It's not that those models weren't there before; after all they didn't all just simultaneously race out of the showrooms. They were probably out there for a while, but you simply didn't register seeing them. Now that you're aware, you see them everywhere.

expand your awareness to see those around you as members of your network as well, you can refine your networking focus.

Focus on networking. Practice honing your networking focus until it becomes a highly developed skill. Begin by:

- Asking yourself if people you know, meet, or hear about could help you network.
- Clarifying precisely how these people could help. For example, could they introduce you to the mayor, recommend you for membership in the garden club, or inform you where they found their antique Venetian carnival masks?
- Asking who of the people you identified could help you the most and/or connect you with the best.
- Finding out what places and events would be worth attending to expand your contacts.
- Questioning how you can make the best use of information to connect you with your targets.

Developing networking focus isn't difficult, and, before long, it will become second nature. Work to get it down pat, because the ability to focus sharply is a priceless skill that will bring you rewards for the rest of your life.

Listening

Learn to listen and observe. Most people love to speak, so let them carry the conversation. While they speak, pay careful attention to what they are saying. If you let them speak, most people will be revealing. They will disclose who they are, what they do, and what they need. And, if after listening, you're still not sure, ask them directly. Show your interest and be attentive.

Ironically, when you listen, people will think that you are interesting. They will be flattered because you gave them your attention and showed interest in them. They will consider you a wonderful conversationalist simply for listening to them.

When you're with interesting people, listening is fun. After all, we already know who we are and what we've done, but we don't have the same knowledge about others. Listening is the best way to find out and to make strong connections.

When the conversation turns to you, answer briefly and then turn it back to the other person. Let him or her be expansive. Ask questions that will encourage them to continue. Questioning is an essential component of listening. Inquire about anything you don't understand, need to know, or want to understand in greater depth. Questioning helps to increase your understanding and knowledge about what you heard. Ask three questions about them, their product, or their service and you'll lay the groundwork for a solid relationship.

Taking Inventory

In order to maximize your networking opportunities, you must know who is in your network. Check your address book, the business cards you've collected, and those scraps of paper filled with names and numbers. Ask yourself who else you know who would make a great network partner. Determine whether those with whom you interact would fit into your network.

Your Network Inventory

Sharpen your focus by making a written list of your network members. Don't overlook anyone! Make your network broad and all-inclusive. Titles and positions can be deceptive and not indicate an individual's abilities, connections, or value to your network. Include people whom you like and whom you enjoy being with and being associated with.

On your list, write next to each name the reason you included that person on your list. Be specific.

Quest for the Best

As automotive marketing guru James Ziegler was waiting for a flight at Atlanta's airport, he spotted Leo Mullin, CEO of Delta Airlines, with a group being photographed for Delta's magazine. Ziegler had always wanted to meet Mullin, but decided not to introduce himself as Mullin was obviously busy. Soon after, Ziegler noticed Mullin walking with Bill, a mechanic for Delta and a friend of Ziegler's from his adult Sunday school class. A few minutes later, Mullin walked over to Ziegler and introduced himself. He and Ziegler talked for about twenty minutes and exchanged business cards before Mullin returned to the photo shoot.

Bill came by shortly after, and only then did Ziegler remember that several months before he had mentioned to Bill that he would really like to meet Mullin. Since that day at the airport, Ziegler has had a direct link to Mullin. Although he has never contacted Mullin to leverage the relationship, he occasionally sends complimentary notes after receiving outstanding service from Delta employees. Ziegler says that he would have no hesitation contacting Mullin, when appropriate, and believes that he could count on Mullin's help.

Generally, those you list will fall into two categories:

1. *Direct contacts (first generation contacts).* These are people who have what you want and can give it to you directly. For example, your objective may be courtside tickets at Madison Square Garden, the names and contact information for media that cover fabric design, or a meeting with your U.S. senator. On your list, write down your precise objective. Then prioritize the names of your direct contacts according to their ability to deliver what you need.

2. *Intermediary contacts (second generation contacts).* These people can introduce you to others, or influence others, who can deliver or lead you to your objective. Intermediaries usually can't provide your ultimate objective, but they can make introductions, write recommendation letters, and move you closer to your destination.

   You should prioritize the names of your indirect contacts according to the ability to connect you to the best people.

Your Personal Inventory

Next, inventory your personal assets to identify what you can bring to the table. To find your personal assets, think about all the things you do well and enjoy doing, classes or training you've taken, awards you have won, jobs you've held, skills learned, accomplishments achieved, and clients/customers satisfied. Don't overlook "intangible" qualities such as determination, people skills, capacity for hard work, honesty, reliability, humor, kindness, taste, sensitivity, and compassion. Jill likes to point out that, "Intangibles like personality, laid-back style, judgment and willingness to accommodate can be the key to making great matches."

When compiling your personal inventory, you should identify your talents, skills, and values.

- *Talents* are your natural attributes. Some lucky souls sing beautifully, while others can dunk a basketball or mentally calculate long rows of figures.
- *Skills* are the capabilities that you have acquired: Web site design, fine-furniture making, or antique bookbinding.
- *Values* are the objectives that you consider to be important: high earnings, creativity, recognition, or working in teams.

Remarkably, few people can identify their own talents, skills, or values even though they play a crucial role in their behavior. When you approach people, they're interested in benefits; they want to know what you can do for them. If you've identified your talents and skills, you can more clearly articulate the benefits that you can provide and see how it fits into different situations. Instead of informing a network contact, "I'm an office administrator," you can explain that you can keep a business running smoothly by handling hiring and firing, supervising staff, scheduling, ordering, bookkeeping, and billing.

The most important factor in building strong relationships is that the parties share common values. According to career transition coach Randy Block, "The most important linkage in a networking situation is that you and your network partners share congruent values." Think about it; it makes good sense. People prefer to deal with those who share their values. For example, if you like stability, working under pressure, heated competition, or living on the edge, you're probably going to be happier being with those who feel the same.

In the past, values were seldom discussed. However, when people who are connected share common values, bonds can be forged that can lead to strong, productive relationships. Common bonds make relationships work; they put people on the same page. So, if you're trying to make a good match, focus on the other party's values.

Think about your values. Look back on situations in which you had fun; were happy, successful, and proud; and made money. What did you like most about them that you would like to replicate?

When you've identified your talents, skills, and values, you will feel more confident because you recognized precisely what you have to offer and the values that make you happy. Your self-knowledge and confidence will increase your ability to clearly communicate, which will boost your appeal. Instead of vaguely asking network contacts if they know of job openings, your approach will be stronger when you say, "This is what I'm good at; these are the benefits I provide. Do you know of anyone who can use my talents?"

Helping

Radio personality and bestselling author Mike Litman believes that the best way to create new relationships is by going first. "Leaders go first," he observes, so help others before asking them for help. "People have gold mines of resources and contacts, but they don't open up their treasure chest until you go first."

"Helping is the best form of networking," Stephen Burgay, Senior Vice President of Corporate Communications for John Hancock Financial Services, advises. "The key to building a network is establishing good relationships with your network members. You need to get to know them and wherever possible, help them out long before you need them to help you." If you help, those you helped will pick up your call and they will be more willing to assist you.

The ideal time to build your network is when you are in a position to help others and you don't need their help. Or as President John F. Kennedy advised, "The time to repair the roof is when the sun is shining." Burgay calls this "implicit networking" because you have no agenda. In contrast, "explicit networking is when you have an agenda such as needing a job, wanting to change jobs or being on the move."

Implicit networking builds goodwill and can position you for tomorrow. Help others whenever you can because it might motivate them to assist you when you need help. For example, if you have a job, assist whomever you can and don't worry about receiving anything from them in return. If you lose your job, you may want to call upon those you helped. Had you not helped them, they may be less inclined to assist you since you're no longer in power. However, they may fulfill your request in gratitude for past favors. Usually, you need networking most when you're no longer in a position of power. So give early to build relationships that transcend changes in your circumstances.

Give generously and gladly. Give more, not less, than is expected. Don't just fill expectations—exceed them—exceed them beyond your contact's hopes. Mike Litman calls it "going the extra mile," which means extending yourself and doing as much as you can. "Giving to get," he points out, "is not giving, it's bribery."

Prospective clients frequently contact Rick before they are ready for his services. He tells them that he would be happy to take their money, but—at this time—it would be wasted. Rick directs them to experts who can provide what they need and get them ready. Much later, many call Rick and say, "I called you two years ago and you wouldn't take my money. Everyone else was dying to get their hands on my money, but you insisted that I get all of my ducks in a row. Well, now I'm ready and you're the only one I'm calling because you sent me in the right direction and wouldn't rip me off."

You should never give resentfully or sullenly as if your arm was being twisted; always be gracious. Don't brag or broadcast your generosity to others or repeatedly remind those you helped of your largesse. Be generous in spirit and deed and, when

> **Free Samples**
> To build your network, give your product or perform your service for free to the right people. Write it off to goodwill; consider it an investment. Usually, people are more willing to try things that are free and will remember when they receive something of value, especially when it comes at no cost. The object is to get your product or service out there, to let its quality speak for itself and to impress those who are in a position to help. If it's really good, your contacts will spread the word and endorse you, your product, or service.

possible, be anonymous. Create an example of generosity that others will admire and be encouraged to follow. Giving generously and gladly can create a circle of helping, giving, and sharing that will assist others and that you can remain a part of long after your power and influence have waned.

Getting Organized

Now that you've identified the members of your network, create a system that will always keep you current. Create a detailed network database on your Rolodex, Palm Pilot, or address book or simply start a separate card or computer file. Also investigate the numerous computer programs that provide contact-organizing services. They include ACT!, TeleMagic, Goldmine, and tons more. Think of the members of your network as your stock in trade, your inventory. Keep detailed records of your stock of network members and review them regularly.

Collect as many names as possible because you never know when a contact could lead you to the perfect fit. Successful networkers collect business cards and contact information as if it was money. A contact whom you have barely met may have heard about you, been impressed by you, or think that you or your product/service are fabulous and want to hook you up with his or her network.

Rick divides his contact database into three groups.

- *A Group*—His top, most important network members. The people whom he feels could help him the most.

- *B Group*—Other, less important contacts whom he has actually met.

- *C Group*—People he does not know but has heard of, seen, read articles by, and would like to meet.

Become a collector. Gather lots of information about your contacts; list their awards and accomplishments and note them in your records. This information can be the icebreaker that softens contact and makes him or her want to help. It can also assist you in positioning yourself. For example, when you know that an elusive contact is a breeder of champion pugs, you might want to read up on pugs or attend some dog shows.

Get into the habit of collecting business cards and making notes. Carry a small notebook or a personal digital assistant, such as a Palm Pilot, at all times to record names and pertinent information. Keep notebooks and writing implements in your car, briefcase, purse, boat, and near all computers and phones.

Ask everyone you meet for his or her business card and give yours in return. On the back of their cards, jot down where and when you met them and what you discussed. Each night, when you empty your pockets, briefcase, or purse, toss the cards into a receptacle that you assign exclusively for your collection of contact information. Then set aside a specific time each week, like 9 A.M. each Monday, to transfer information from the cards to your network database.

Review and update your network database on a regular basis. Update all changes as soon as they occur. At the least, scan your database once a month and go over it from top to bottom every three months. The more familiar you are with your list, the more easily and quickly you will be able to link network contacts when the need arises.

You Are Your Product

Regardless of what service you provide or product you produce, remember that you *are* your product. In networking, you are always onstage. People will watch you with a critical eye and take notice of how you act. If people like and believe in you, they will extend themselves on your behalf, and they will speak highly of you to others. People who trust you will give preferences to you, your products, or services—preferences that will make your life much easier and your profits much greater.

However, if people don't like, believe in, or trust you, they won't help. They may not say "no" to your face, but when it comes time for them to deliver, something will always divert them and you won't get what you want. And once doors close, they become much harder to reopen.

Start locally. Move from your street, to the neighborhood, the town, county, state, and on to a national level and the world. Build a solid support base and continue to branch out. When you venture into bigger and deeper waters, maintain and keep in contact with your base.

Starting Close to Home

In building your network, it usually makes sense to work from inside out. When possible, build initially upon those who are nearest and dearest to you. Then inch your way toward others who aren't as close. First lay a foundation of those who:

- Are closest to you and who know you best.
- Have the best connections.
- Can provide or bring you closer to your objective.

Close contacts, especially family and dear friends, often have a high stake in your success and will go to greater lengths to link you up with contacts who can help. Often, your near and dear ones will be more willing to go out on a limb for you, contact powerful people, or call in chits that they've obtained in return for past favors. In addition, they might recommend other helpful contacts or strategies.

Be expansive; define your "nearest and dearest" liberally. Don't look only to your parents, siblings, and close friends. Contact your aunts, uncles, grandparents, distant relatives, in-laws, godparents, and your business associates and members of their families. Explore all connections. Ignore the "removed" with relatives who are "once removed." With friends, call upon their parents, siblings, relatives, friends, and business associates. Leave no stone unturned.

Remember that:

1. The easiest and most efficient way to expand your resources is to tap into your sources' resources.
2. The smartest place to start networking is with those who love or owe you.

So whenever possible, begin your networking close to home. Develop a plan, have patience, build a solid foundation, and work from there.

After you've established your local network and have moved to greener pastures, try to retain your connections with your local contacts. Jill says, "Consider your local network your

Quest for the Best

In his marvelous book, *Dig Your Well Before You're Thirsty*, Harvey Mackay relates TV personality Pat O'Brien's networking story. At the University of South Dakota, O'Brien was a student of Dr. William O. Farber, chairman of the Political Science Department and a master networker. Since South Dakota is so isolated, Farber decided to build a network that would help his students extend their reach. In his network, Farber joined forces with powerhouses such as Al Neuharth, founder of *USA Today*; Phil Odean, CEO of BDM; Ken Bode of *Washington Week in Review*; U.S. Senator Tim Johnson; former Senator Larry Pressler; and two federal judges.

When O'Brien told Dr. Farber that he was interested in pursuing a broadcasting career after graduation, Farber contacted another former student, Tom Brokaw. Brokaw was then the news anchor at the NBC affiliate in Los Angeles and made one phone call that got O'Brien a job at NBC in Washington, D.C. Two days after being a student in South Dakota, O'Brien was working for David Brinkley, a giant of news broadcasting, in the nation's capital. Because of networking he was able to launch his long, highly successful career in broadcasting.

base, your bedrock supportive structure. Try to find time to return to meetings of local organizations and to attend local events. Those who helped you on the way up will appreciate and spread the word about your unwavering support."

Identifying Hurdles

Before you begin to network, examine possible roadblocks that could block or delay your success. At each networking stage, anticipate what could derail your efforts or prevent you from reaching your goal. List all that could go wrong. For example, before you call a potential target, plan what you would do if he or she refuses to take your call. Should you send a note, e-mail, or sit on his or her doorstep? Should you ask another network contact to call or should you just abandon your efforts and place your attention on another target?

Identifying possible hurdles enables you to easily handle many of them when they arise. It also can alert you to problems or insurmountable flaws in your plans before you've spent time, effort, and energy or embarrassed yourself. Anticipating obstacles can also force you to develop more realistic and feasible strategies. Finally, it can help you determine what additional assistance you may need and how much that assistance is worth to you.

Promises, Promises

Most people mean well. When you're together, they're warm, friendly, and brimming with encouragement, compliments, and helpful advice. They have a million ideas as to what you should do and how you should do it. Some may reel off the names of your heroes and claim that they are closest buddies. They may even volunteer to call someone at the top of his or her field, which would put you on the map and solve all your problems. Well, don't hold your breath!

Some people are big talkers or shameless name-droppers. Usually, the name-droppers are easy to spot. When most contacts make promises to you, they will sincerely want to help. However, other pressures and demands have an uncanny way of disrupting the best of intentions. Unfortunately, the old saying, "Out of sight, out of mind," is frequently true, and many contacts, no matter how sincere or well-meaning, simply don't come through.

So take every promise with a grain of salt, not as a guarantee or sure thing. Give it the same weight as you would a stock tip from a stranger. Until proven to the contrary, accept that your contact's promise was well intentioned and made with a true desire to help. Build on his or her good intentions. Salvage something positive from your contacts' promises and from their failure to deliver, but never show annoyance or irritation. Don't try to shame or blackmail those who failed you into helping you. They will resent it and your methods can easily backfire.

In the face of disappointment, work to keep the avenues of communication open with your contacts, strive to build goodwill, and position yourself to fight another—and hopefully, more productive—day.

Action Steps

1. List the names of five direct contacts and state the reason you listed each.

   _____

   _____

   _____

   _____

   _____

2. Provide the names of five intermediary contacts and state the reason you listed each.

   _____

   _____

   _____

   _____

   _____

3. Identify below your talents and skills in the order in which you're most proficient. Think in terms of benefits that you can provide rather than job titles or descriptions.

_____

_____

_____

_____

_____

4. State your values in the order of their importance below.

_____

_____

_____

_____

_____

Four

Setting Your Priorities

THIS CHAPTER WILL COVER:

Types of introductions

Identifying your purpose

Avoiding confusion

Creating a compelling vision

Networking events

Prioritizing

"I'm always looking for people
who do a better job than I can."

—T. Boone Pickens

Networking starts with introductions and introductions come in a number of forms. For the purposes of this book, we have separated them into five categories:

- Cold calls
- Leads
- Cold introductions
- Warm introductions
- Personal introductions

Cold calls are attempts to contact people whom you don't know and have little or no information about. They can hardly be called introductions. Calling names that you received from telephone directories or similar listings are cold calls. They are usually attempts to contact targets whom you don't know without any introduction or referral. Most of the irritating, impersonal phone solicitations we all receive are cold calls.

Leads, as used in this book, are names that usually fit a common profile, such as men between ages twenty-five and thirty-five, self-employed carpenters, or mothers with more than three children. Those who give you leads may not know the people included on lead sheets or lists. Frequently, the names on lead sheets are compiled by list services and similar sources. For the purposes of this book, leads are simply names without any other type of referral. When you contact a lead, it's little more than a cold call.

Cold introductions are more personal leads. For example, when your friend Bill tells you to, "Call my cousin Sally, she may be looking for someone like you." Get permission from Bill to mention to cousin Sally that Bill suggested you call—or else your call will have the same impact of a cold call from a stranger. Without Bill's permission, your call is little more than a lead.

Warm introductions occur when Bill phones cousin Sally and tells her that you will be calling. If Bill praises you, his introduction will be even warmer. Warm introductions usually give you a better, more enthusiastic reception and it may spur Sally to jump the gun and call you. Warm introductions give you immediate credibility and cousin Sally is likely to accept what Bill recommends. So when a contact gives you a lead or a cold introduction, ask if he or she could call first to turn it into a warm introduction.

Personal introductions occur when Bill personally introduces you to cousin Sally. He may arrange for the three of you to

Quest for the Best

In June 1974, when Bob Iger was a weatherman in Ithaca, New York, he went to New York City to look for a job. He visited his uncle there, who was recuperating in the hospital and was sharing a room with an ABC executive. Iger's uncle asked the ABC exec if he could help his nephew get an interview, and the executive set up an appointment for Iger to meet with a member of his staff. Iger got a position as a studio supervisor and started on July 1, 1974. In 2000, after many years of outstanding work, Iger was named as the president of the Walt Disney Company, ABC's parent company.

lunch together, bring you to Sally's office, or introduce you at an event. Warm introductions carry the message that "this is someone good, someone you should know or use." Therefore, they are the most desirable introductions and what you should try to obtain.

Identifying Your Purpose

Before selecting targets, clarify in your mind exactly what you want. Be specific. Do you want to find someone who can help get your kid into Harvard? Do you want to hire a wedding videographer who also takes black-and-white still photographs? Or do you want to learn how to start an organic garden with drip irrigation? When you are not completely clear about your purpose, you can't explain what you want to others.

Don't make your contacts guess; don't waste their time. Tell them exactly what you want, and be specific! Even close friends, who truly want to help, will lose patience if you are not clear and specific—after all, they're not mind readers.

When you fail to request precisely what you seek:

- You risk getting less than you want.
- Your lack of clarity opens the door for misunderstandings.
- You will probably be disappointed with the results if your request is misunderstood.
- You will still be obligated to return your contact's favor.

To reduce the possibility of misunderstandings, explain what you want in easily understandable language. Never assume that network members, no matter how bright or accomplished they are or how many degrees they hold, understand buzzwords, technical language, words of art, or occupational-specific terminology. Keep it clear and simple. Remember, your objective is to clearly communicate, not to confuse or try to impress.

Avoiding Confusion

We all go through times when we are unsure or vague about what we want. It happens to everyone. Usually, it occurs when our ideas have not crystallized and we have not fully researched or thought them through. Frequently, we only know that we need a job, would like to attend college, or find a place to live, but we haven't settled on a specific career, particular colleges, or acceptable neighborhoods. In many cases, we have not yet identified the steps we should take to reach our goal. We may know that we need help, but we are not sure what kind of help we need, nor who can help us.

At this point, many quit; they make no attempt to move forward. Others take some action, but play it by ear without a plan. They put the cart before the horse because they delude themselves into thinking that they will recognize the "right thing" when they see it, which isn't always true. It's hard to see the "right thing" when you don't know what you're looking for.

Rick always stresses that networking requests must be specific. "Specific requests enable you to communicate more clearly. When targets quickly understand your request, they are more likely to deliver what you need or promptly refer you to others who can. When you are uncertain, your targets will also be uncertain and less able to deliver what you want. When well-meaning contacts are forced to guess what's what, it's usually a disaster. Most of the time, confused contacts do not provide any real help, their valuable time is wasted, and they will be reluctant to extend themselves for you in the future.

"Networking works best when you request help from targets who are well-connected experts in specific fields. If you haven't identified your purpose, how can you identify the best targets? So when you deal with experts—people who are the best at what they do—be prepared, know exactly what you want and how to ask for help."

If you are unclear about what you want, figure it out before you go any further. Use the space below to compile a list that will help you define your purpose.

Make a list of:

1. Your ideal: the best possible job, college, home, etc., that you could desire.
2. The factors that make it your ideal; list the factors in order of their importance. For example, if you got that design job, you could work from home, help out with the kids, and save some childcare costs.
3. Your bottom line: the least that you will accept.

Examine your list to determine whether your wishes are realistic. If they are unrealistic, determine what you could do to make them viable. Could they be attainable if you had more training, experience, or time? Are the shortcomings things that you could or want to overcome? Do you have better alternatives? Is it worth it to you?

Also ask whether the factors that shaped your ideals are otherwise attainable. If so, decide whether it would be easier, wiser,

---

Express What You Want

Remember that the top people are virtually always pressed for time. So, when you approach them it's crucial to know exactly what you want and to express it clearly. If the expert doesn't immediately realize what you want, you may get a quick rejection. Once you've been rejected, you will not only have lost the opportunity to get help from a valuable contact, you've probably lost that person as a contact because the rejection will make it harder, if not impossible, for you to approach him or her again.

or more rewarding to pursue those options. In your analysis, you may find that certain factors are more important to you than your ideal. In that case, it may be wiser to adjust your ideal.

If, after completing this exercise, you can't identify your purpose, seek guidance. We've all been lost, confused, or just stuck in ruts. Most of the time, a good talk or two with close friends, family members, mentors, and business associates will help you work it through. But sometimes, the ruts are just too deep. In that event, consider contacting professionals who are in the business of providing expert guidance and advice. Consider their fees a sound investment in your future.

Creating a Compelling Vision

Business success coach and author Caterina Rando takes the concept of identifying your purpose a step further. She teaches that to succeed, you must have a compelling vision. Rando believes that your compelling vision must be so powerful that it rouses you out of bed in the morning and propels you through the day.

According to Rando, you must see and feel your vision. She recommends picturing yourself at the point when you have achieved your objective. For example, close your eyes and actually see the mayor dedicating your sculpture in the park, waiters serving your apple strudel at the Four Seasons restaurant, crossing home plate in the World Series at Fenway Park, accepting flowers at the Metropolitan Opera, or exchanging vows with the man or woman of your dreams on a tropical South Seas island. See it in full color on a huge Imax screen—smell the aromas and hear all the sounds. Put yourself in the picture.

To be achievable, your compelling vision must have a powerful emotional component. In other words, you must feel it with passion, hunger, or need. Strong emotions are the fuel that powers and sustains your quest; they underlie the commitment that drives you to attain your dream.

People respond to ideas and enthusiasm; they rally around them and support them. People at the top are often visionaries and innovators who will identify with and respond favorably to your ideas, creativity, and passion. To achieve success, your desire to fulfill your vision must be stronger and more alluring than the obstacles you will face in trying to achieve it.

Networking Events

"Any time people get together, I consider it a networking event," Rick declares. "I use the term loosely, and don't restrict it to conventions, conferences, workshops and the usual stuff. The thing is you always have to be ready, otherwise you may overlook terrific networking opportunities." When you attend networking events, however you define them, your purpose must be clear. In most cases, it's to get exposure or make contacts for business, nonprofit, philanthropic, social, or family reasons. When you go to a Chamber of Commerce mixer, Book Expo, or a Sierra Club meeting, you're generally hoping to meet or hang around people who attend these events. Similarly, when you go to a café that caters to musicians, you want to meet or spend time with musicians or music lovers.

Before attending networking events such as conventions, conferences, association meetings, and mixers, ask yourself:

- Why are you going?
- Who will be there?
- Whom do you hope to meet?
- What do you know about them?
- What do you hope to get from them?
- What is the best way to approach them?
- How can you reciprocate?

When you answer these questions, conduct more research to be better prepared. Use the Internet, as it's a mother lode of terrific information that is easy to access. Preparation will improve your focus and your prospects of making the event more productive.

Jill always sets a goal for the networking events she plans to attend; in fact, she sets two goals. The first she calls her "go for" goal, which is a hopefully high figure that would make the event a rousing success. The second is her "promise," the realistic figure that she needs to reach in order for her attendance to be cost effective. Jill then sets a firm figure on the number of new people she wants to meet. When lists of attendees are available, she reviews them beforehand and identifies a set number of particular people she intends to meet.

She also presets the amount of business she hopes to transact as well as the amount of new business she hopes to attract. Jill sets these figures in dollar amounts and puts them in writing. When Jill attends networking events with close friends, she tells them her goals, which boosts her incentive. It also gives her a partner because when friends know her goals, they usually push to find leads and contacts for her. As we will discuss in a later chapter, Jill measures each month by whether or not she met her projections.

Be Open to Opportunities

When you go to that café that caters to musicians, or to the ballet, aquarium, or a PTA meeting, networking is seldom your primary motivation. However, networking opportunities can always arise at non-networking events. Since the best contacts can be made in the unlikeliest, most unplanned-for situations, you must be alert to all networking opportunities and be prepared to react. You also must take pains to act appropriately.

Even the most casual meeting can be an interview or an opportunity. We've all heard millions of stories of how someone profited from being in the right spot at the right time. However,

Quest for the Best

Food stylist George DoLese was biding his time in a long line at a New York City pastry shop when the man behind him started talking to him. Initially, the man complained about the long wait, but both he and DoLese agreed that the pastries were worth it. The conversation then moved on to pastries and food in general. As DoLese reached the counter, the man handed DoLese his business card. He was the executive chef at a restaurant owned by Donald Trump and had an opening that he thought would be ideal for DoLese. DoLese called, got the job, and had an amazing experience working for Trump.

these bonanzas aren't simply the product of dumb luck. True, people may have been fortunate to be where they were, but they also had the ability to provide a good impression and to make the best of the opportunity.

However, reacting to perceived opportunities in non-networking situations can be tricky. Although it might be tempting to jump on opportunities that present themselves during school board meetings, it may not be worth the risk of offending others in attendance. Inappropriate networking can be disruptive and impolite. It can sully your reputation and alienate people who could help you somewhere down the line.

So be alert to networking opportunities at non-networking situations, but pursue possible contacts only if it feels 100 percent appropriate. Don't make a move if you have the slightest doubt. Usually, it's simply a matter of timing and since networking is not the primary reason for your presence, the best approach is to wait for a break or until the main business has concluded to pursue your quarry. Then make contact, exchange business cards or contact information, and arrange to call or meet at a later date. If making contact might be at all awkward, uncomfortable, or disruptive, save it for a more appropriate time.

Often the best networking tactic is to concentrate on the situation at hand rather than attempting to make network contacts. By focusing on the business at hand, you can demonstrate your abilities and dedication to the cause. As a result, others will usually be impressed and want to get to know you better. So concentrate on your purpose in being present and contribute. Build your reputation and the contacts will follow.

Prioritizing

Select your targets precisely and limit the number of targets you pursue. Instead of trying to saturate large groups, initially concentrate on reaching a few key people and identify who can best provide concrete help. Often, when you try to cover everything, you end up handling nothing well.

Quest for the Best

Writer, speaker, and trainer Dave Sherman gave us a great example of why he is called "The Networking Guy." In February 2003, a good friend of Dave's was laid off from her job of eight years and needed to quickly find other employment. She contacted Dave, who first identified what she was looking for and then sent an e-mail to his 2,600-member network requesting their help in finding a job for his friend.

In less than twenty-four hours, Dave received well over 200 e-mails and at least twenty-five telephone calls with offers to help his friend. From the responses, she learned about over eighty job openings, many of which were good jobs with great companies. If she had not known Dave, it could have taken her forever to reach that many contacts. In less than a week, Dave's friend landed a great new job at a bank that offered her better pay and better benefits than her last job. That is the power of networking!

You should choose a few realistic targets and focus on them. Identify potential targets and research them thoroughly. List those in the order of who you think are the best. Find out everything about them and become expert on their strong points, passions, weaknesses, interests, aversions, hobbies, families, background, habits, histories, and connections. See how they link with your strong points, passions, weaknesses, interests, aversions, hobbies, families, background, habits, histories, and connections. What you learn through your research will give you insights on how to approach them and how to build and maintain a rewarding relationship when you've connected.

Make sure that your targets have the ability to provide what you want. Remember that you have limited time, resources, and energy; if you try to cover too much you could squander your valuable assets. When you have too many targets, it's difficult to give each the attention it deserves, so concentrate on reaching the best. When you have too many balls in the air, it takes only one misstep for most of them to fall. So target precisely because you don't want to waste your precious time pursuing the wrong people or attending irrelevant meetings.

Remember to be realistic. Don't shoot for the brightest stars unless you have a realistic chance of reaching them. Even then, examine the feasibility of approaching every target cautiously.

Powerful people surround themselves with multiple layers of protections that are specifically designed to keep the uninvited away. To reach them, you have to circumvent electronic fences, which can be time-consuming and frustrating—like sitting forever on hold and being treated coldly. And when you reach celebrity targets, they may not deliver. So don't waste your time trying to go where you're not wanted. If you have a strong lead, pursue it, but expect resistance. When you feel strong resistance, politely say, "Thanks," move on, and focus your efforts on Target Number 2. In a similar vein, the best doctor, restaurant, or building contractor may be booked when you need him or her. When your choice is not available, move to the next best.

Building Slowly

Connect the links. Review your network roster and find connections on which to build. Link your connections like a set of steps that will lift you to higher floors. Start with small steps; build and be patient. Prepare for a slow, steady ascent. Don't rush.

Carefully select targets whom you know, whom you can reach, and who can deliver what you need. Start with those who will be happy to help you. Although your close contacts may not be able to deliver as much as celebrated authorities, they are more likely to actually provide what they promise. So start with them and build steadily.

As you grow and make new contacts, build upon them at each stage. Concentrate on developing a reputation for quality, expertise, and honesty; become well respected and well known; then people in power will approach you. Move slowly, incrementally, and steadily.

Narrowing In

Selecting networking targets is always risky. People and businesses are often not what they seem. Even after the most detailed, probing examinations, certain information never comes to light. Many ingredients are involved in matchmaking. Some of them are hard to measure and others are intangibles or personality based. Although there is no foolproof formula for choosing targets, the following questions could eliminate some of the risk:

1. Does your target provide products or services that could affect you or your business?
2. If so, how?
3. Who are your target's customers?
4. How do your target's customers fit or relate to your customers?

5. How do your customers and your target's customers overlap?
6. What geographical area does your target's products or services cover?
7. Who are your target's competitors?
8. How can you help your target?
9. How can your target help you?

Don't be blinded by titles or purported accomplishments. Titleholders may just be flunkies and lack the clout to deliver what you need. Often, those who received credit may not be the ones who actually did the work.

Line Extensions

To make connections, Jeff Kahn, Chief Strategic Officer of Ruder Finn, Inc., suggests using line extensions to map your route. If you want to get to Dr. X, make a list of all of the information you've learned about him through your research. Then draw a line from Dr. X through your network contacts until you find connections.

Here are some steps you could take:

1. Examine your network membership list and identify who might lead you to your target.
2. Ask network members if they know Dr. X, if they have contacts who excel at performing delicate cardiac valve surgery, or if they know of people who have suffered from heart valve problems. If so, contact them.
3. Spread the word widely. Let everyone in your network know your objective and your target.
4. Ask your network members if they have contacts who work in health care and insurance and, if so, get in touch with their contacts.

5. Check with the doctors' hospitals, local medical associations, your insurance agent, and even your lawyer.

When you identify targets who are the best, they may be beyond your reach. Trying to contact them directly is often impossible, so investigate whether you can reach them through intermediaries. Also, consider Ken Glickman's suggestions for contacting those beyond your reach in Chapter 6.

Go National

Many local networking organizations are branches or chapters of national organizations. Become active with local groups that have state and national organizations. Start locally and then expand to the state, national, and international levels.

When you join a group, attend regularly. To make meaningful contacts, you have to go to more than one or two meetings. Become a recognized presence. Volunteer for committees to demonstrate your abilities. Organization members come and go and groups, on all levels, are always searching for fresh, new talent to fill empty slots. Making a name for yourself on the local level is a wonderful stepping-stone to nationwide prominence.

Before you travel to another market, investigate whether the organizations you belong to have branches in the cities you plan to visit. If so, check if they will be holding events at the time that you can attend to expand your network contacts.

For example, Jill is active in the San Francisco chapter of eWomenNetwork. Last spring, she was booked to speak in Houston by the National Speakers Association. As soon as she had that booking, Jill called the eWomanNetwork chapter in Houston and asked if they needed a speaker at the time she would be in Houston. The Houston chapter then booked Jill to speak. Even if the Houston chapter hadn't asked her to speak, Jill—dynamic networker that she is—would have attended

the local chapter meeting or lunch to meet and network with
Houston chapter members.

Action Steps

1. State your purpose, and identify exactly why you want to
   network.

   _____

   _____

   _____

2. Describe in full, graphic detail your compelling vision.

   _____

   _____

   _____

3. Pick three targets and draw line extensions.

   _____

   _____

   _____

4. Write down three ways that you can inoffensively network
   at non-networking events.

   _____

   _____

   _____

Five

Finding the Best

THIS CHAPTER WILL COVER:

Researching your targets

Implementing a step-by-step plan
for reaching the best

Deciding who is best

Moving fast

Circumventing handlers
and protectors

"Surround yourself with the best
people you can find, delegate
authority, and don't interfere."

—Ronald Reagan

When selecting potential targets, think first in terms of categories. Do you want to connect with the best surgeon who specializes in repairing cardiac valves; the best moving company that safely transports valuable, delicate art works across the country; or the top automobile mechanic who can expertly repair vintage Mustang convertibles?

The names of people whom you could contact may immediately come to mind when you identify your category. They may be folks you know or have heard of. They may have gone through similar problems, are close to others who had

The Best Lead to the Best

To identify the best people, turn to the best. The best people usually know and work with the best. Assume that the CEO of your company, the head of your congregation, or the owner of the best restaurant in town knows or uses the best accountant, security specialist, or maintenance service. Explore your network contacts to find out who might be able to reach them or direct you to others who could.

the same needs, or are involved in the field or category that you identified.

For example, if you need an estate planner, you may think of someone in your network who (1) was recently involved in the settlement of an estate; (2) is, knows, or works with top lawyers; or (3) is, knows, or works with life insurance professionals. Get in touch with your network contacts, ask them who they consider to be the best, and if they can't identify the best, ask if they know others who can. Then contact the people they name.

Researching Your Targets

Frequently, you may discover that you don't have network contacts who can help you find the top practitioners in your areas of interest. When this occurs, the best approach is to conduct lots of research. To find the best, organize your research like a military operation.

As part of your basic research, gather background information by reading books, articles, newsletters, and Web sites about your area of interest. Learn as much as possible about your potential targets and their fields, and focus on possible interests or activities that could provide connections.

To identify and learn about the best potential targets, check the reference section of your library and especially business, university, and grad school libraries. A number of publications that can be found at most libraries can help you find the best. They include:

- *Who's Who In America* (Marquis Who's Who) provides information on the top people by name, geographical area, and professions.
- *International Who's Who* (Europa Publications Limited) is *Who's Who* on an international scale.
- *Who's Who* and similar publications also publish volumes

that cover specific fields, including finance and industry, politics, theater, art, American women, and writers.

- *The Yearbook of Experts, Authorities and Spokespersons* (Broadcast Interview Sources, Inc.) is a directory listing experts in various fields that media personnel can contact to obtain authoritative information on news stories.
- *Current Biography Yearbook* (The H.W. Wilson Company). H.W. Wilson also publishes *Current Biography (www.hwwilson.com/currentbio/curbio.html)*, a monthly magazine that includes eighteen to twenty profiles each issue.
- *Forbes Richest People* (John Wiley & Sons, 1997). Provides short profiles that lists each individual's worth, source of wealth, family status, and business history.

In addition, special issues of *Forbes* magazine annually include lists of:

- The World's Richest People
- Best Paid CEOs
- 400 Richest Americans
- 100 Top Celebrities
- The Best Places

If you live in a major metropolitan area, you should check out the magazine for your city. Often, local publications such as *New York* or *Boston* magazine have annual "Best of . . ." lists. It's a great resource for finding the top people and places in your community.

Note the names of individuals listed, profiled, and quoted in publications and how they can be reached. If contact information is not provided, get it from the publication. Communicate with the authors of the pieces you read and ask them who they consider the best people. Explain to them the reason you're interested and exactly what you're looking for. Writers who cover specific businesses can be immensely helpful because they generally know the best people, are objective, and are willing to

An Educational Experience

Approach the research process as an essential learning experience. Consider it a prerequisite for any important undertaking. Go about your research diligently because it will give you a greater overall understanding of the subject and problems that might arise. As you research, set priorities. Identify your goals in the order of their importance. Zero in on what you should be looking for and don't waste time with whatever you should avoid. The information you gain from your research will also make it easier for you to talk with, interview, and deal with experts, which usually pays off.

help. If they don't respond, understand that writers, especially those with large and national publications, are frequently too busy to even take time to eat lunch.

The next step is to mine your network. Cross-examine your network partners to obtain the names of, and information about, the best potential targets. Create a system or plan and follow it through. Work your way up; your network partners may not know the best experts, but they could refer you to other practitioners who could lead you to the best.

Reaching the best is usually similar to climbing a ladder. The ladder is your plan; it must be in place before you climb. Otherwise, you will never get off the ground. When the ladder/plan is firmly set, you must take one rung at a time until you reach the level you want to reach.

Step-by-Step Planning

In order to find the best, proceed in an order similar to the following.

1. Interview for personal recommendations

It's usually best to start by speaking with network contacts who have gone through the experience that you are about to encounter. Contact those who have actually hired people in the areas you are researching. It will save you valuable time and energy! First, approach network partners upon whom you can rely—people who have high standards or values similar to yours. Often your friends and business associates will have worked through similar problems and can refer you to people who can help. If they can't, ask them if they know others who might be able to help. You will be surprised how often they will have leads—and those leads will move you in the right direction.

Don't expect to get the names of the best people right off the bat; it can take a while. Think of the first people you ask as starting points. Be patient and prepared for a process that requires you to speak to a number of individuals before you even begin to get helpful information.

Cast your net widely by getting the word out to everyone. Seek assistance from your entire network and beyond. Ask your network partners to question their network members. Solicit recommendations from as many people as possible. Remember that the most unlikely contact could connect you to your ideal, so cover all the bases and don't fail to explore any potential source.

"Ask, ask, ask!" Rick stresses. "One person is going to lead to another and to another and so on until you collect enough information to identify the best. You never know which one is going to be the gold. And if you ask your friends and contacts to give you two or three names, one of those names could be the one who will make the difference."

The act of simply asking for help can get the ball rolling because when good friends and great networkers don't have answers, they usually dig deeper. They will adopt your search as their own. They will ask their friends, family, and network members for recommendations, which they will forward to you. When personal recommendations or references identify someone as the best, specifically ask the following questions and be sure to get satisfactory answers:

- Did the expert get the job done?
- Rate the quality of performance on a scale of 1 to 10.
- Did he or she deliver at the agreed-upon price? If not, why?
- Was what he or she provided acceptable? If not, how was it deficient?
- Was the individual accessible?
- Did he or she return calls? If so, how promptly?
- Did he or she provide understandable responses to questions?
- Was he or she pleasant to work with, supportive, or simply all business?
- Did they know others you could contact and can you use their names?
- Would you use/hire that individual again?

When prospects whom you might hire provide you with references, personally check them out. Call all references and listen for hesitation, reluctance, or conviction in their voices. Ask prospects for their client/customer lists and contact a random sample of those on the lists.

2. Make use of business contacts

In your search for the best, obtain leads and information from members of your network who supply, service, and do business with people in the fields that interest you. If none of your network partners has such connections, ask him or her to check with members of his or her network who may be able to make the connections for you.

Suppliers and vendors are a rich source of information. They often have close relationships with the major players in their fields. From the goods and services they provide, they are

A Warning
Keep in mind that suppliers and vendors may have ulterior business reasons for their recommendations—referrers often do. They may lack high standards, be impressed with a smooth operator who pays promptly, and have no knowledge about performance features that are vital to you. When you receive referrals and recommendations, always factor these considerations in as a part of your decision-making process.

aware of the type, size, and quality of the projects that the best people are pitching and on which they are currently working. They can tell you exactly who to call and what to say.

If you are looking for the best photographer for your annual report, speak with printers, suppliers of paper or photographic equipment, graphic designers, advertising people, and magazine designers. Those who work in the same or allied businesses can identify the best and usually can connect you with them. The mere mention of your contacts' names can often get you past electronic barriers that make so many top people so hard to reach.

3. Go where they ply their trade

When possible, visit the scene of the crime—the prospects' places of business—to observe them in action. Often, you may not be able to fully understand what you see, but you could obtain interesting and important information. Visiting a place of business reveals much about a person: his or her style, taste, lavishness, frugality, sense of order, organization, neatness, and much more. Any of these items could impact your working relationship and should be factored into your decision.

Before you enroll your kid in a particular school, visit it. Speak with teachers, staff, and some students. See how they are dressed, and how they behave and interact. Observe the degree of control, formality, casualness, order, or laxity. Visit at times when you are not expected. Talk to graduates, parents of students, and former students who did not graduate. Try to draw information from a broad cross-section that will give you an accurate reading.

Don't expect the hospital to allow you to watch a surgeon transplant a heart. However, a hospital visit may provide you with the opportunity to speak with nurses, interns, or other staff members who can offer crucial information. They usually work with a great many surgeons and may have strong, well-founded opinions regarding which ones are the best. Similarly, you can't hang around the garage while a mechanic rewires an old Camaro, but you can gather a consensus from some pros at the shop who know about cars as to who could best replace your one-of-a-kind Citroen's upholstery.

4. Explore industry, trade, and professional associations

Many industry associations have referral services. You can find a local dentist through 1-800-DENTIST and most professional associations will refer you to practitioners who specialize in various areas. At best, their recommendations are leads, nothing more. They give you the names of people who can help, but those whom they recommend are not necessarily the best. To find the best, you need reliable recommendations from sources you trust.

Industry, trade, and professional association members in your network can usually identify the best, and they can probably provide you with warm introductions. By reading association bulletins, newsletters, press releases, Web sites, and other information, you can obtain the names of major players. Also, these materials can give you insights into the top people, their knowledge, positions, reasoning, and clarity of expression. Information that you read can also provide you with good openings or approaches for reaching them. For example, after reading a compelling article by or about an individual, you could contact him or her to compliment or comment on the piece, ask about or outline your problem, or schedule an appointment.

Associations have lots of committees and are always looking for volunteer help. By volunteering, you can meet and work with important figures in the association and make invaluable contacts with the best. Volunteering can also help you rise within the association and attain positions where the best people will court you.

Local associations meet on a regular basis, as do most regional, national, and international associations. These events have social components. Check meeting schedules in the association's newsletter or Web site or with a network member and drop by. Check the program to see which people are making presentations or are on panels. While you're there, poll some of the members on their opinions regarding whom they consider to be the best.

5. Ask at schools and universities

Teachers and professors are often the leading experts and authorities. They also can identify the best people, at least by name. Teachers and professors have read and often contributed to or consulted on their schools' publications. They also require their students to read works written by top people. Many of the best who are not full-time teachers also teach. They hire students as assistants and interns. They write for school publications and enlist help from students on works they are writing. Often, experts are also active in alumni associations, donation drives, committees, activities, and special projects. Check your network for members who are affiliated with schools and universities. They may be able to identify and introduce you to the best people or send you to others who can.

As we previously explained, to play in the networking league, you must be prepared to give something in exchange for each contact's help. In Chapter 3, we asked you to inventory your personal assets. We requested that you list what you could provide to reciprocate for your target's help. Review that list and if you haven't completed it, please do so now before continuing further.

Quest for the Best

When Dennis Crow of Pierce & Crow, a leading high-technology executive search firm, began his business, he had a strong background in high-tech operations, but no executive search experience. So he called upon social friends and business contacts including those who had invested in his former business. Crow told them about his new business and asked if they would introduce him to key people in their businesses.

One contact, a partner in Silicon Valley's most powerful venture capital firm, invited Crow to his office where they discussed Crow's plans and prospects. At Crow's request, the venture capitalist agreed to send a letter introducing Crow to his business buddies. Crow drafted a letter, which his contact edited, put on his letterhead, and sent to forty-four of the who's who of the venture capital community.

Within six weeks, Crow had forty-four appointments. Not only did he meet forty-four top high-tech executives, but virtually all of them had the venture capitalist's letter sitting prominently on their desks. Although it took time and hard work to get their business, Crow credits the letter for jump-starting his business and getting it launched.

Deciding Who Is Best

Deciding who is the best, or who is best for you, is always subjective; however, there are some basic guidelines that can ease the dilemma. Weigh your determination on the:

1. Quality of the recommendations you receive. Ask yourself if you can rely on those who vouched for the expert. Do you trust their opinions? Was their situation parallel to yours and, if not, should the differences matter? Rate your comfort with their referrals on a scale of 1 to 10 and ignore any recommendation that is not at least an 8.

2. Corroboration. Although the quality of recommendations should outweigh the number of endorsements you receive, it's always helpful to have a strong consensus that supports your decision. When your decision is important—like finding a top surgeon, tax attorney, or business broker—ask around and get as many opinions as possible so that you can arrive at an informed, well-reasoned decision. Again, rate your comfort with the corroborating recommendations and ignore any that are not at least an 8.

3. Your instincts. If you have strong feelings or are uncomfortable with what seem to be mountains of clear, irrefutable evidence, trust your gut. Our instincts are not merely irrational feelings, but are deep signals that are a product of our experiences and data we have collected throughout our lives. At the least, they should be carefully considered because you may have a sound reason for your feelings, but not be able to clearly articulate it. Similarly, question yourself when you quickly feel totally comfortable with a decision. View your reaction as if it was a childhood crush or an infatuation. Investigate further, more deeply, and be cautious to make sure that you weren't simply blinded by a pretty face, a polished line, and celebrity status.

To select the best, Jill usually tries to get three recommendations. Then she chooses the one that feels right. "When you contact several potential sources, you usually get a sense of who would make the best match for you. You can also sense who won't work or whom you don't want to work with, which is really important," Jill observed. "Of course, when you know someone who repeatedly directs you to the best, then that may be the only person you need to call, but those people are rare," she cautioned. "Usually, you need to contact different people for different things."

When you aim for the best, start locally. Identify whom you know and determine how they can get you to the top. Plan an incremental approach. Get to know neighborhood association members and then move up to your supervisor, alderman, town councilors, mayor, state representatives, governor, U.S. senators, all the way to the White House. All the while, keep learning and building your knowledge base so that when it's combined with your contact base, you will be more desirable. And remember to remain in contact with those who helped you as you move up.

Moving Fast

Occasions often arise when you need the best right now. You don't have the time to move from contact to contact, do extensive research, or wait—for example, when health is concerned. When you or a loved one needs a heart valve repaired, you don't want to settle for just any surgeon, you want the best.

Usually, the referral process begins with the cardiologist, who diagnosed the faulty valve. He or she will give you several names. Then it's time to turn to your network. If you've laid the proper groundwork, the process should go smoothly. If you've got top people in your network whom you can immediately access, you should be able to move fast.

Immediately, get the word out and tell everyone you contact to spread it widely. Call network members who are in health-related fields and tell them, "I'm trying to find the best surgeon who specializes in repairing cardiac valves." Ask if they know the surgeons that the cardiologist suggested or have heard of them. Tell everyone that "time is of the essence" or "this is an emergency."

If your inquiries are unsuccessful, broaden the search to other members of your network and ask them to contact their network partners. Often, they will give you the names of others who might help.

Handlers and Protectors

According to Rick, "People at the top are often the nicest people. They're usually warm and delighted to help, but everyone is afraid to talk to them. Most of them understand how hard it is to reach the top; they've been there and have insights that can fast-track your ascent. The problem is that many of them have handlers and protectors who are hired to keep people at bay; it's the handlers' job to shield their bosses. The handlers are usually the ones who are impressed with themselves and the trick is to avoid them and get to their boss."

Jerry Horn, the right-hand man for the author Anthony DeStefano, told Rick the following story. When he was seeking endorsements for DeStefano's new book, *A Travel Guide To Heaven* (Doubleday), he zeroed in on top celebrities. One of his main targets was Quincy Jones. After sending a copy of the book, Horn called Jones's office and was emphatically told by Jones's assistant that there was "No way Quincy will endorse your book. He has no time and he doesn't do book endorsements." Horn politely thanked him, expressed his understanding, and hung up. The following day, Horn called Jones's office again and was directed to the assistant. "I thought I made it clear that Quincy will not endorse your book," the assistant roared. "Wait, just listen to me," Horn interrupted. "I simply wanted to thank you. I've been trying to get endorsements from many famous people and I've been dealing with assistants who have been stringing me on for months without delivering. You're the only one who said no straight out, right away, with no BS and I really wanted to thank you for saving me time and being so professional." The very next day, Horn got a call from the assistant saying that Jones read the book, loved it, and would be delighted to give it a glowing endorsement, which he did.

Action Steps

1. Identify three categories of network partners you need.

_____

_____

_____

2. Set forth four criteria for finding the best.

_____

_____

_____

_____

3. Name three people whom you can rely on to direct you to the best.

_____

_____

_____

4. List the people you would call in an emergency when you need a doctor, lawyer, plumber, and computer servicer.

_____

_____

_____

_____

Six

Positioning Yourself for the Best

THIS CHAPTER WILL COVER:

Becoming an expert

Declaring your expertise

Going beyond your level

Getting yourself there

Seminars and workshops

Getting published

Getting creative

"Network everywhere and with everyone. Don't wait for a special occasion to enjoy the benefits of networking. You never know where you will make a connection that can change your life."

—Melissa Wahl, Executive Director, National Association for Female Executives

Networks are built around the exchange of information and networking is information intensive. To be both successful and sustaining, networks must constantly receive an influx of new and relevant information; information that network members can take, analyze, and then parcel out to their network partners who then can make the best use of it.

To efficiently utilize the stream of networking information requires knowledge—expert knowledge. First, it requires the knowledge to understand the full implications of the information received and what it means. Second, it requires knowledge about the members of your network, their needs, capabilities, and capacities. With this knowledge, members who receive information can then analyze it, determine who can best use it, and allocate it to those network partners who can benefit from it.

So, to build and maintain the best network, you must become an expert. The more knowledgeable you become, the more desirable you will be to potential network partners. Your pretty face, clever wit, and winning personality may initially get you noticed, but you will fade as fast as last month's news if you don't have an expertise that others desire.

By becoming an expert, you will make yourself more attractive to those who can give you the greatest help—the "in" crowd, the movers and shakers, the decision-makers and the power brokers. Those at the top, the best people, want to associate with the best. They want to do business and socialize with the best, and so should you. The surest route for reaching the top is by becoming an expert in your field.

Your expertise is the exchange that you give back to your network partners in return for their help; it's your ticket to the dance. Being an expert simply means that you know what you're doing. It doesn't necessarily mean that you're the world's most recognized authority, although you may be. It also doesn't mean that you know absolutely everything about your field . . . no one does! But it does mean that you're one of the best.

When you're acknowledged to be an expert, people want to hear what you have to say. Invitations to participate in meetings, panel discussions, workshops, and conferences pour in. You will be asked to write about your expertise, enter your work in competitions, and contribute your efforts for charitable causes. These opportunities will give you exposure, terrific PR, extend your influence, and introduce you to community and industry leaders. In addition, you will be coveted as a speaker, teacher, and competition judge, which will introduce you to bright talents, who will extend the demographic of your network to a younger generation.

Expertise is always with you. If you were awakened in the middle of the night and cross-examined about your area of

Added Value

Your expertise enhances your value to your network. Each area of expertise adds special flavors that make your contributions to the network desirable and unique; they give your contributions added worth. For example, your ability to operate a home-based office may prove invaluable to a network member who just left a large corporate job to start a new business in his or her garage.

interest, despite being groggy, despite being extremely cross, you should be able to rattle off all the right answers on the spot. When networking opportunities arise, you possess the information and have the expert knowledge that you can use—and you must be prepared to showcase it.

Be alert to opportunities to demonstrate your expertise and be prepared to capitalize on them. Don't abruptly or inappropriately force your expertise on listeners, but be patient. Wait for appropriate openings when what you have to say will be relevant and further the conversation. Learn to bide your time and listen to what others are saying. Then, when and if opportunity knocks, move fast because it may not come again.

Rick believes that the biggest mistake networkers make is not waiting for the opportune moment. "So many people are impatient and don't wait for others to finish speaking," he says. "They interrupt and force themselves upon people. By doing so, they take a potential positive—a wonderful networking opportunity where they could establish a good contact—and turn it into a negative. People consider them rude and feel that they think that their agenda is the only one that matters."

Hold back until you see a clear opening. Understand and acknowledge that your target is busy. Rick suggests saying, "Excuse me for bothering you. I promise that I'll only take thirty seconds of your time. I am a pushy PR guy, I'm a pain in the butt, but I can help you if you just give me a little of your time."

"They don't know who you are," Rick explains. "So disarm them by making light of yourself. It breaks the ice. Show that you understand their situation and sympathize. Say, 'I know you've had a horrible day' or 'you look exhausted so I promise I'll only take thirty seconds.' Also let them know, right off the bat, that you're not going to waste their time, that there will be something good in it for them. It's important to make them feel that you're not just a 'user' and that there's something tangible that they can get from you."

Quest for the Best

Ken Browning, a prominent Beverly Hills entertainment attorney, tries to help his clients whenever he can by introducing them to his extensive contacts. At one time, Browning represented a well-known celebrity who was featured in an infomercial for a major cosmetics company. While representing her, he developed a business relationship with a management executive for the cosmetics company. Several years later, hairstylist Nick Chavez asked Browning to become his partner in developing a line of hair care products. Browning connected Chavez with the cosmetics company, which showed great interest in his line, but the company ultimately decided to go in a different direction.

A few years later, the cosmetics executive became the Director of Beauty at a cable-shopping network. Browning asked her if she would be interested in selling Chavez's product line through her network. As a result, Perfect Plus, the Browning/Chavez Company, went on the network, where it sold out its initial offering in record time and became the network's bestselling hair care line. Today nine years later, Perfect Plus is a highly successful company. The success of Perfect Plus also boosted Browning's law practice by attracting a steady stream of companies that sell their products via infomercials and home-shopping outlets.

Research New Members

In your quest for knowledge, learn as much as you possibly can about your new contacts and your network partners. When you identify people you would like to meet, or after you meet new people, find out as much about them as you can and become an expert on them. Discover what they do, what they like, what they dislike, and what they need. Get information about their families and backgrounds. Discreetly ask them about themselves, get them talking. Also ask your network partners about them.

The more you know the people you meet, the better your chance of building a relationship with them. Find common denominators, and shared experiences or interests. Know where their kids go to school, their special charities, and their hobbies. Then, be patient and wait for the right moment to say, "I hear you are a competitive swimmer, so am I," "I loved your article on artichokes. Will your recipes work with potatoes?" or "Where are your favorite places to find mid-century modern chairs?"

Note when a contact mentions that she is involved in boating or wants to get her kids into a drama camp. Then train yourself to look for published items about those interests and send them to her with a brief note, "Thought this might interest you." Use your knowledge about your contacts to connect them with business contacts who could help them. Finding leads for network partners is an essential part of networking. In order to hook your partners up with the best potential matches, you need to know what they want and need:

- Question your network partners about their interests
- Visit their places of business
- Discover what they want
- Find out what they need
- Ask how you can help

Learning about your network partners also has the secondary benefit of broadening your knowledge, exposing you to and teaching you about new areas. These new areas could help you in the future and send you in directions that would be impossible to presently imagine.

In Chapter 3, we asked you to inventory your personal assets. Now, review that list and prioritize your personal assets according to what you consider to be your greatest strengths. In reviewing the list, pinpoint the contributions you can provide to individual members of your network and how they would support their goals. In your review, also ask how you can adjust what you can contribute to suit particular situations or enhance its value and increase its demand.

Ask everyone how you can help. Rick tries to end every e-mail he sends by asking the recipients how he can help them. The mere offer breaks down barriers and helps build mutually beneficial relationships. Plus, he loves to help!

Declare Your Expertise

Tell others about your expertise and why it's so special. Find ways to promote yourself by writing articles, giving talks and demonstrations, starting Web sites, joining groups, and participating in conferences, workshops, and discussions. Volunteer your services to build your reputation and impress people who may be in a position to help you. Write or talk about tasks that you've performed a thousand times: how to write a press release, how to barbeque ribs, or how to care for tropical fish. Teach others, step by step, how to do it. Here are some tips for making your expertise known through writing:

- Write articles. Prepare two written versions: one 1,500 words and the other 800 words. Be ready to recite them on short notice.
- Always have copies of both articles on hand to distribute.
- Keep your articles simple and don't state everything you know. Cover no more than seven points, no less than three.
- Make your articles practical, not theoretical: "How to Write a Movie Review," "Five Easy Steps to Weight Loss," or "How to Make Seamless Welds That Last."

Send your articles to publications, organizations, Web sites in your field or related fields, and to your network. Follow up with e-mails or phone calls. Offer yourself as an expert speaker. Recite your article aloud as speeches. Prepare visual aids such as slides, illustrations, and charts. Practice your presentation on your family and friends. At the end of articles, include your bio and state who you are, what you do, how you can be reached, and your message. Prepare a more extensive bio that can be distributed during your speaking engagements.

Testimonials and Endorsements

Reap greater rewards from your accomplishments by obtaining testimonials and endorsements. Business expert Mitch Axelrod maintains that, "Word of mouth is still your best advertising. Most people don't take full advantage of the word of mouth benefits they can get from their clients. The most powerful marketing tool is not what you say, but what others say about you. So get testimonials and endorsements from your customers and clients. People pay attention to them. They are the highest, most specific and deepest praise you can get." Here are some steps to follow:

- Ask each of your clients/customers for a letter of praise.
- Ask them to state how great your work was and how much they enjoyed working with you. You'll be surprised how highly they praise you and how well they express it.
- Ask for endorsements as soon as the projects are complete.
- Ask your clients/customers to write your testimonials on their stationery and tell them to hold them to two or three paragraphs.
- Ask each client/customer to give you the names of three friends or associates who may be interested in your product or services. Ask if you can use their name, and

better yet, if they would be willing to call or write their friends recommending you or to introduce you to them in person.

- Accumulate endorsements, build your own personal collection; they're invaluable for getting business.
- Explain to clients/customers that you plan to post the testimonials on your newsletter, Web site, and promotional materials.
- Point out to your clients/customers how their testimonials could help them by increasing their visibility.
- If clients hesitate, offer to prepare drafts for their editing and approval.
- Update Web sites regularly to add recent testimonials and to remove those that are dated. However, run a few old testimonials because they show that you have a long track record of customer satisfaction.
- Carry copies of your testimonials and endorsements whenever you might have a chance to get new business.

When you want to buy a book, do you look at blurbs endorsing the book? Most people do; that's why so many books include them. When you are reading the blurbs, are you influenced by the praise given by endorsers you respect or like? Does it enter into your decision to buy the book? Endorsements work, especially when they are from top people whom others trust. So request testimonials from the best, most respected, and trusted people you can reach.

Letters to the Editor

Show your expertise by writing letters to editors and by posting comments in Web chat rooms. Write letters to editors on local issues in which you have a great interest or some experience. As a result, members of your community will quickly learn

---

Valuable Associations

People like to deal with the best. It builds their confidence because they believe it improves their chances for success. Being associated with the best is prestigious and gives your contacts something to crow about. Our world is star-struck and celebrity driven. How many times have you heard friends say, "Guess who I just saw?" And then they proudly reel off the name of some celebrity whom they passed on the street. Those who are considered the best or stars in their fields can charge more and there is greater demand for their products and services.

---

your name, positions, and expertise. Well-reasoned articles and comments will also help you build a following, promote name recognition, build your stature, and in short extend your network.

Moving Beyond Your Level

All too frequently, the people we want to meet, those who could quickly catapult us into the stratosphere, are beyond our reach. Not only do we not know them, but we don't know anyone else who can reach them. Calling them blindly without a warm introduction is futile and e-mail seldom works. Occasionally, an e-mail will slip through, but it's a long, long shot.

To reach the unreachable, you must cultivate the relationship, and even that may not work. The best plan, according to professional speaker and marketing consultant Ken Glickman, is sending personal letters. The chances of succeeding remain slim, but one of your letters could touch a responsive chord and yield rewards.

Glickman suggests writing a personal letter that states, "I've followed your career (read your book/article, saw your interview) and respect what you are doing. I wonder if there are any books that you could recommend to me that had a major influence on your life or career." Most powerful people won't respond, but some just might.

If any of the people you write do respond, read the book or books they recommend and when you've finished it, send a brief note saying, "I read the book and found it very useful. Thank you very much." Keep it brief. Just say thanks and nothing more. Let it go at that and move on.

If, thereafter, your career advances—you get recognition, an award, a better job, a promotion, or a good raise—then send another note saying, "I just wanted you to know that I was promoted or did _____ and want to thank you. I attribute a great part of my success to _____, the book you recommended." You can leave it at that or ask him or her to recommend another book.

This technique keeps you in touch, lets your contact know that you're doing well, and helps you build a relationship that could turn into a deeper, mentoring relationship. At the same time, it builds name recognition and creates a favorable impression. If, somewhere along the line, you meet this powerful person you will have established a solid basis on which to further the relationship.

Get Yourself There

Put yourself in places and positions where the magic can occur. As Woody Allen is reputed to have said, "Eighty percent of success is showing up."

"Schedule yourself to be in the right places where you can meet the best people," Jeff Kahn, the Chief Strategic Officer of Ruder Finn, Inc., advises. "I've met at least a third of the people who became my good friends or people who became my business customers in the first class airline lounges or in business class plane seats. Choose your gym not just because of its equipment, but also factor in the people you will meet there and interact with."

Kahn, who is in public relations, works out in a gym frequented by celebrities and policy makers. "The interactions at the gym forge bonds that are stronger than those created at terse business meetings because they're based on shared experiences. They go beyond just transactional or business dealings. Every choice you make—where you work out, where you eat lunch—creates opportunities. If you have an idea where you want to go in life, then those choices will create better opportunities for you," Kahn stressed.

Get out of the office or the house and expose yourself to people and experiences that can move you in new and exciting directions. Relinquish some of the control that may keep you

Quest for the Best

When super graphic designer Marta Salas-Porras was a student at Art Center College of Design, the students majoring in differing disciplines seldom mixed. For example, graphic design students and transportation design students kept their distance. Salas-Porras, however, was intrigued by other disciplines and found herself spending considerable time with students from the automotive and industrial design departments. Not only did the processes and materials involved in automotive and industrial design play a major role in shaping Salas-Porras's career, but a student she met from the transportation design department introduced her to his childhood buddy, whom she later married. "The most important thing is to get yourself out there," Salas-Porras advises. "Be curious, explore other areas, put yourself in positions where you learn. If you want to grow, don't just stay in the same old place. When you expose yourself to what's new and different, you never know what you'll learn and where it may take you."

languishing in the same old place, repeating the same task, and making the same mistakes. Expose yourself to opportunities because you never can predict what might happen.

Watch out for comfort, as being comfortable can be a trap. It can keep you in bed, in the house, and in the same old same old where it's hard to progress. Comfort can stymie growth and keep you treading water. Although we all work to be more comfortable, comfort can be a trap. So, break old habits, break the mold, take chances, do something daring, and try something new.

Seminars and Workshops

Seminars and workshops are ideal for increasing your expertise and building network contacts. Attending can:

- Polish your skills
- Bring you up to speed on industry developments
- Introduce you to new areas
- Help you meet new people
- Establish you as an authority
- Put you in contact with other authorities
- Help build your network

Seminars are great for networking because everyone is in the same industry or has the same basic interests. When you have common interests, networking becomes far easier and more natural. Introductions and explanations can be shorter or even eliminated because the joint experience of learning, asking, and problem solving in your own field takes over and creates a bond.

At seminars, you can meet, learn from, and forge relationships with renowned experts and your peers. The leading experts are easy to identify and more approachable than you might think. As a student you can feel a sense of camaraderie and sharing with your peers that enables you to make new friends, friends who can become network members. Often your new friends will be from different areas, which can extend your reach and help you to grow.

If the benefits of attending seminars and workshops are good, the rewards from leading or teaching them are stratospheric. Leading or teaching seminars and workshops helps you network by increasing your visibility, reputation, and stature. It positions you as an important and respected authority as well as a leader in your field. It makes you the subject of more attention, and if you're good, of more respect. As an acknowledged authority, you can extend your influence so that you can meet and network with others on or above your plane, the authorities at the top of your field.

When you lead seminars and workshops, you get to demonstrate your expertise to attendees who are eager to hear what you have to say. As a leader, you can exchange ideas and help solve problems with the top minds and the most successful players in your field.

Both Rick and Jill frequently give workshops and seminars. It enables them to meet lots of interesting people, share their knowledge, and learn from stories and information raised by those who attend. Their participation also enhances their visibility and helps maintain their positions as two of the top leaders in their fields.

Create Your Own Seminars

Appearing at seminars is so desirable that the competition between speakers is brutal. If you're not in demand as a speaker, volunteer to help at other events. It will give you exposure to important and powerful people, position you as an insider, and teach you how to operate workshops, seminars, and other events.

After apprenticing for a while, you may be ready to create, organize, or lead your own seminar. Running your own seminar can be extremely lucrative and let you make invaluable contacts. It will also enable you to assess whether you enjoy operating seminars and if you do it well.

Start small, learn on the job, and work your way up. Establish a track record for excellence. Starting small also limits your financial risk. Identify topics that can draw large audiences. If you're a professional ballet dancer, run a seminar to show mothers of aspiring dancers what the career entails; if you're a real estate agent, teach people how to buy houses and secure mortgages; and if you're a psychologist, teach stress reduction techniques. Give practical, hands-on, how-to instructions so attendees return home with tangible benefits.

In the beginning, don't charge but rather offer free seminars, or just cover your costs. Consider what you learn from the experience as ample compensation. Plus, you will be building a following because those who enjoy the event will return, be your supporters, and join your network. Try to convince a local charity, religious, civic, or social group to allow you to use their facility in exchange for a modest contribution and/or publicity. If that fails, rent a room.

To promote your seminar, call upon your network. Print posters and fliers and have your network members help you place them in high traffic areas such as schools, universities, community centers, libraries, and businesses in or related to your field. Send announcements to local radio stations and related Web sites. Get names from your network, mailing lists, and local organizations. Send postcards or fliers announcing the event. Promote your seminar on Web sites. Send e-mails to your network and ask them to send it to their networks.

Service Clubs

To get experience, start with local service clubs. They are perfect venues for making and learning from mistakes. Local

A Warning
Running seminars can be difficult, demanding work. Instead of trying to operate your own, you might consider offering your services as a lecturer to organizations that sponsor such events. Unless you've got a big reputation, don't even think of starting at the top. Instead, begin by volunteering your services to local organizations and then, as you gain skill and recognition, moving to bigger, more prestigious events.

service clubs are equivalent to comedy clubs where comics, both experienced and novice, go to polish their material and try out new routines. Give yourself the freedom to make mistakes and learn from them.

Volunteer to speak at events sponsored by the Elks Club; the Rotary Club; the Veterans of Foreign Wars; the Chamber of Commerce; Women in Business; religious, business, and civic groups; and so forth. Don't ask to be paid; just chalk it up to your education. Consider these opportunities to perfect your presentation, build your reputation, and meet potential customers/clients, contacts, and the media.

Keep in mind that certain local organizations appeal mainly to retirees or to a demographic that might not interest you. While events sponsored by these groups may provide opportunities to sharpen your presentation, they may not be the right places for you to network. So when you book engagements, factor in the audience profile.

Get experience, build a reputation, and network by teaching a workshop or even a course for local educational institutions such as community colleges or adult education programs. Participate in online conferences. Approach businesses that provide adult education and career-development courses.

Conferences and Conventions

With the exception of *Oprah*, the *Today Show*, *Larry King Live*, or your own infomercial, conferences and conventions are the top way to position yourself. Speaking at major conferences puts you at the pinnacle of your industry and provides unlimited networking opportunities. At conferences and conventions, the presentations are ostensibly about learning. In reality, they're equally about networking, socializing, and fellowship.

If you get the chance to speak at a conference or convention, become a performer. Spice up your presentations with humor, anecdotes, and real-life stories. Everyone loves inside scoops about people, companies, and gossip in their business. Update the latest industry developments. Focus on a few hot topics that people in your industry should learn and cover them expertly. Encourage questions from the audience. Make yourself available after you've completed your presentation. Run off copies of news developments, articles, examples, reading lists, and abstracts of presentations so that attendees feel that they're getting value.

Get Published

To increase your credibility, your profile, and your attractiveness to networkers, it pays to get published. Being a published author gives you the elevated status of being an authority.

You will likely have to start out by writing articles in your field (often for little money) in order to gain the experience and track record that will enable you to have a book published. Having a book with your name on it is a particularly powerful networking tool because:

- Authors are respected and sought after.
- Giving a copy of your book to a potential network member or target can tip the scales in your favor. It creates instant

goodwill and writing a personalized message will thaw the most glacial prospects and convert total strangers into grateful, loyal, long-standing devotees.

• Once your book is published, your status as an expert becomes permanent and can never be taken away. You're listed in the Library of Congress, in the Copyright Office, and with Amazon.com. The local media competes to interview you; you get cool invitations and attract conference groupies. Being a published author is exciting and satisfying . . . its fame lasts far more than fifteen minutes!

• The exhilaration of authorship is addictive. Once published, virtually all authors want to repeat the experience. Subsequent books reinforce their status and further their careers. Public admiration and respect is intoxicating.

• Most authors don't make very much money from selling their books, but their books help propel their careers. Their books establish them as authorities and consequently they can charge more for their goods and services. They can also begin lucrative consulting careers. And, you never know, there's always a chance that your book will make the bestseller list, and you'll appear on Jay Leno and David Letterman and hit the jackpot!

Get Creative

You should always look to find unusual ways to distinguish yourself and to stand out from the crowd. Use inventive, creative approaches to show targets and potential network partners that you're someone with flair, vision, imagination, and a great sense of humor. Think boldly and give people a laugh. Everyone loves a good laugh; it lowers their guard and makes them more receptive.

Design your business cards, brochures, literature, and Web site to attract positive attention. Examine the profile of the targets you want to reach and determine the looks and approaches they like. Identify the styles that are standard for your groups. Build on their standards, but play with them, and push the envelope.

Test the waters before going public. Bounce your ideas off your friends and network partners and heed their feedback. It's easy to go overboard and get lost in playfulness. Always keep in mind that your objective is to attract favorable attention, not to come off as a fool or a clown.

Creative approaches pay dividends; they make delightful stories that are repeatedly retold. Since these stories center around your creativity, they portray you in a glowing light and add to your legend. Upon hearing these stories, others will admire you, remember your name, want to meet you, and spend time with you. So unleash your imagination, and become creative.

Quest for the Best

Author Randy Peyser was growing desperate. Her landlords had just informed her that they were giving the great little cottage she had rented for the past six years to their daughter. Finding new housing that would accept Randy and her old Springer spaniel, Cookie, was proving impossible, so Randy decided to get creative. She made a sign that said, "RENTAL NEEDED, INQUIRE WITHIN." She taped the sign across the front of her T-shirt and went to a giant picnic that was attended by several hundred people.

Randy's sign was a big hit at the picnic; it gave everyone a good laugh. A woman approached Randy and said that she had a room in her home to rent. Randy explained that she had a dog, but the woman replied, "Oh, that's not a problem, I love dogs." Randy checked out the room, liked it, and moved in. Although she only expected to stay for a few months until she found a larger place, Randy and Cookie lived there happily for nearly two and a half years.

Action Steps

1. Name three ways that you can declare your expertise.

   _____

   _____

   _____

2. Identify five customers or clients who can give you written testimonials.

   _____

   _____

   _____

   _____

   _____

3. List three individuals that you admire, but are beyond your reach, whom you will write letters to.

   _____

   _____

   _____

4. List several subjects on which you might be able to write articles or a book.

   _____

   _____

   _____

   _____

Seven

Your Networking Toolkit

THIS CHAPTER WILL COVER:

Strong sound bites that
draw attention

Writing your sound bite

Delivering your message

Descriptions of you,
your product, or service

Business cards

Address lists, calendars,
and writing materials

"My networking magic formula is to
make contacts to get contracts and
multiply my exposure to source, serve
and motivate everyone I encounter."

—Mark Victor Hansen,
bestselling author

When you call professionals to repair a major appliance in your home, they bring the right tools to handle the job. Similarly, the best networkers are always equipped with the tools they need to do a great job. The networkers' toolkit consists of:

- A fabulous sound bite
- A great description of you, your product, or service
- Business cards
- An address list
- A date book
- Writing materials
- Expertise

Picture yourself entering a room that is packed with strangers, all talking intently in tight little clusters. As you walk in, you scan the room hoping to spot a familiar face, but there is no one you know, not a single soul. So you head toward the table piled high with snacks trying to look confident and hoping your jitters subside. As you're walking, you try to figure out your next move, but then your eyes make contact with a pleasant looking chap standing to your right. Talking with him are two nicely dressed women. As you draw closer, he turns toward you, sticks out his hand, introduces himself, and beckons you to the group. The women smile softly, say hello, state their names, and extend their hands. And presto, you're smack dab in the middle of a conversation with three total strangers.

After a few opening niceties, one of the women looks you squarely in the eyes and inquires, "What do you do?" Although it's said pleasantly, you can sense her intensity, and you can tell that she's all business. You realize that she is really asking, "Who are you and why should I spend my valuable time talking with you?" which is a really good question.

At that moment,

- Do you have the right answer?
- Do you know exactly what to say?
- Do you have a killer sound bite ready to reel off for just such occasions that can transform a perfect stranger into a network ally?
- Have you practiced that sound bite so that you can flawlessly rattle it off?
- Do you have a great business card?
- Can you give a quick, clear description of what you offer?

Sound Bites

A sound bite is your opening, your introduction, your verbal calling card. It's a succinct, memorable, defining statement that explains who you are, what you do, and how you can help. To be a great networker, a killer sound bite is essential. We live in a world where few people have time for the full story. Even at networking events, people are always scanning the room, planning their next move, and seldom giving you their full attention. When they need information, they want condensed versions, digests, or capsules that take only seconds to deliver, are easy to grasp, lock in their mind, and are easy to recall.

It's hard to get people to listen. They're overwhelmed by endless demands. Everyone wants their time and energy. Most of the people you would like to reach can't spare a moment; they're overbooked and overloaded. So, if you get their attention, you better grab it wherever you are!

When you get an opening, you must express yourself:

- Quickly
- Clearly
- Compellingly
- Memorably

Create a sound bite, a descriptive message that you can deliver in less than fifteen seconds when you meet new people. The purpose of a sound bite is to capture your listeners' attention and give them information that will whet their appetite for more. Some refer to sound bites as "elevator speeches," because they are snappy descriptions that can be rattled off in the time it takes an elevator to rise from the lobby to the fifth floor. The more you say briefly, the better the sound bite. As theater impresario David Belasco said, "If you can't write your idea on the back of my calling card, you don't have a clear idea." Rick tells his clients that their sound bite is the opening that gets them to stage two. It's the first impression they make, the attention-grabbing device that will get them, and their message, noticed, remembered, and repeated.

Your sound bite must be a captivating, memorable message that makes contacts stop and listen, want to learn more about you, and introduce you to their friends and colleagues. If it's short and gets their attention, it buys you more time to sell them. Your sound bite must be:

- INTERESTING enough to attract immediate ATTENTION
- POWERFUL enough to be REMEMBERED
- CONVINCING enough to STIR overloaded listeners into action

In ten to fifteen seconds, your sound bite must explain:

1. Who you are
2. What you do and
3. Why you make a difference

Sound Bite Examples

The following are examples of effective sound bites:

1. I used to weigh over 300 pounds. Now, I'm a size 8. I can teach you the best diet to lose weight and keep it off. *(Diet book author)*
2. I help people stay in focus; I'm an optometrist.
3. I show people how to get the best, unlimited free publicity. *(Publicist)*
4. I make investors rich from small investments. *(Investment broker)*
5. I turn your experiences, adventures, and ideas into bestselling books. I'm a ghostwriter. *(Freelance writer)*
6. I make the most delicious, mouth-watering, and beautiful desserts for parties and special occasions. *(Pastry chef)*

If you want to be a successful networker, prepare to vigorously promote yourself. Be ready to blow your own horn in such a way that listeners will remember the tune, but not consider you a blowhard. In the face of intense competition, distinguish yourself from the crowd and the best way to start is with a sound bite.

Writing Your Sound Bite

Before even attempting to write your sound bite, be sure that you clearly know what it is that you do. Most people don't know what they do, according to business expert Mitch Axelrod. "If I ask 100 people what they do, ninety of them will mumble, stumble, and jumble. They've never really sat down and created a statement of what they do that is based on the results they achieved for the people they served," Axelrod explains. "While

Quest for the Best

Several years ago, networking coach Sarah Michel made her "Perfecting Connecting" presentation at a conference of the United States Olympic Committee. At a later cocktail reception, she was drinking a glass of red wine and talking to a woman who had attended her presentation. Curt, a man she had helped with his sound bite after her session, raced toward her, suddenly picked her up, and gave her a big bear hug. This caused Michel's wine glass to spill all over her companion's beautiful cream-white suit.

"I'm so sorry," Curt said, "but you're not going to believe what just happened. After I left your session, I went into the restroom and mentally practiced my sound bite. As I was leaving, another man asked me what I was doing at the conference. Remembering your instruction, I looked this guy straight in the eyes, stood tall, and said, 'I'm here to make some new connections and smoke out new opportunities where I can bring my twelve years of sales and marketing experience in the athletic sports and merchandising industry to a progressive company where I can really impact the bottom line.'"

The man then said to Curt, "I'm the VP of New Business Development for Nike. Would you like to grab a beer and talk about possible opportunities for you with Nike?"

Curt hugged Michel again, thanked her repeatedly, and then gave his business card to the woman in the stained white suit. "Send me the bill," he insisted, and went off to meet the Nike VP.

we think we know what we do, it's only from our own perspective. Our clients often perceive the benefits we provide quite differently. And they, and people like them, are usually the targets we're after."

Ask your customers or clients, "Why did you buy from me?" Ask even if you think you know. Inquire of ten, fifteen, or thirty customers or clients, why did you buy from or do business with me. At first some will be reluctant to tell you, but keep trying. Explain to them that their answers are important to you. The answers you receive may surprise you. They may state reasons that you never would have suspected or imagined. They may also reveal miscommunications, lack of clarity, or just plain omissions or oversights by you.

After receiving your customers' or clients' input, incorporate what they told you into your sound bite. If customers tell you that they do business with you because you always deliver on time, put it in your sound bite. You might say, "I run Al's Automotive Parts, where we always deliver on time." The point is to tell those you meet the outcomes and results you have produced for your clients and customers, not just naming the product you sell or the service you deliver. As a result, your pitch will more clearly explain the benefits that you can provide. It will also prevent listeners from putting a label on you, stopping them from shackling you with their preconceived notions or lumping you in with all the other salespersons, professional speakers, or construction workers they know.

Business coach C. J. Hayden believes that the best way to capture your listener's attention in a sound bite is first to state whom your message is intended to interest. In her sound bite, Hayden starts by saying that she teaches business owners and salespeople. Next, state the benefit you provide, Hayden teaches. Tell listeners what is in it for them before you tell them what you do or how you do it. When you state your title or label first, it can position you in the mind of the listener. Upon hearing titles, many listeners immediately put people in a particular niche or slot and stop listening. If you open by saying that you are a lawyer, a listener might immediately connect you with unpleasant experiences they had with lawyers or with lawyer jokes and not listen to how you can help.

You should always focus on the benefits. When people take the time to explain to others what they do, they typically focus on all the features of their product or service. This response is fine if they want to be like their competition. The only way to set yourself apart is by focusing on the benefits that your product or service provides. It's the benefits that people want to hear about because they are always concerned with "what's in it for them."

Give your sound bite in words that everyone can understand, including those who are not in your industry. First, easily understood terms clearly convey what you want your listeners to hear. Second, in networking, the person you address may recommend you to others and if he or she does not fully understand

What Can You Do for Me?

Speaker, writer, and trainer, Dave Sherman, also known as "The Networking Guy," instructs clients to, "Have an engaging introduction—in this fast-paced business world, people have less than ten seconds to engage others in a conversation. What most people say when asked, 'What do you do,' is the LAST thing they should ever say. Most people respond with their name, their title, and their company name. The challenge with this response is that NO ONE CARES WHAT THEY DO FOR A LIVING. People only care about what their company will do for them. If you can tell people how you can help them in ten seconds or less, you will hear the three most beautiful words in the world, TELL ME MORE!" Sherman notes.

what you said, he or she will not be able to clearly explain it to his or her contacts. Many of those whom you approach will not be in your industry so avoid using words that are specific to your industry; listeners may simply not understand them.

When you are the best, broadcast it and trade on it. Say, "We make the best hamburgers"; "the quietest, or most efficient air conditioners"; or "We provide the best canine obedience training." And be prepared to follow up by explaining why you, your product, or service is the best.

Putting Your Sound Bite Together

Make your sound bite an attention-grabbing introduction. Think of it as a commercial jingle selling you. Work it into letters, mailers, announcements, brochures, ads, e-mail signatures, forms, questionnaires, and applications.

1. First, write the first thoughts that come to mind. Don't worry how long they run or how much space they occupy. Be honest and truthful, but approach it from the bright side. Take your time; make as many attempts as necessary. When you have something down: (A) circle each descriptive word that you've written; (B) then list all of the circled words on a separate sheet; (C) place the listed words in the order of their importance; (D) question whether each of the selected words is the most descriptive and colorful word available; and (E) if not, add or substitute more graphic, illustrative, or hard-hitting words.

2. Draft a sound bite that runs for one or two sentences. Begin with, and give prominence to, the most important words on your list. Although your sound bite should clearly and cleverly communicate your message, clarity is paramount. Don't sacrifice clarity for cleverness.

3. Business Advisor Mark LeBlanc suggests that you avoid the use of humor. "You may get people to laugh, when the real

point is to be clear, congruent, and consistent with your marketing message." However, others disagree and recommend humor, provided it clearly gets your point across.

4. Read the completed sound bite aloud several times and change whatever sounds awkward. Trust your ear. If you repeatedly trip over certain portions, change them to something more comfortable.

5. Underline the key words to be emphasized. Recite your sound bite aloud to test whether the emphasis on those words works. Experiment with differing rhythms and intonations. Recite your sound bite to others and get their input on both the content of your message and your delivery. Consider making changes that listeners suggest. Test it on different groups to get diverse reactions.

6. Recite the sound bite out loud until you believe it and feel comfortable delivering it. When you believe your sound bite, others will also. You'll also sound more confident and convincing.

7. Time how long it takes to deliver your sound bite. If it's more than thirty seconds, cut it to thirty seconds or less, then try to lop off another ten to fifteen seconds without weakening the message. Don't memorize your sound bite, but instead picture the key words and reel them off in order as if you're descending a ladder.

8. Practice your sound bite in front of the mirror, in your car, in the shower. Audiotape and videotape yourself. Concentrate on looking sincere, enthusiastic, and confident, but don't overdo it. Don't act, emote, or be dramatic. Speak conversationally, with sincerity. Don't be a ham or a clown—be professional.

9. Practice, practice, practice—on your family, friends, even your pets. When you deliver your sound bite, imagine that you are meeting the world's greatest networker, the president, Nelson Mandela, Steve Jobs, or Oprah and that your business depends on your being booked on her show.

Quest for the Best

After months of going to networking meetings, having no luck and no favorable responses to his offerings, Business Advisor Mark LeBlanc tried a new method of introducing himself. Prior to this, he felt that he was repelling people with his various methods of introducing his products and services. So on this particular morning, when he got his opportunity, he simply stood up and said, "My name is Mark LeBlanc and I run a company called Small Business Success. I work with people who want to start a business and small business owners who want to grow their business."

The response was overwhelming. A number of attendees responded favorably and within thirty days LeBlanc got seven new clients. The floodgates opened and LeBlanc understood the importance of using the primary outcomes of his work in his sound bite. He now had come up with a defining statement that became the cornerstone of all of his marketing efforts, including his networking meetings. That morning became a turning point in LeBlanc's business!

Delivering Your Message

Maintain eye contact and smile softly when you give your sound bite. Don't force it with some big, artificial grin. Smile warmly and convey confidence, assurance, conviction, and sincerity. Show listeners that you're proud to deliver your message and that you believe in yourself and the benefits you can provide.

Project that you're an expert by speaking with:

- Authority
- Excitement
- Passion

Excitement and passion are contagious. Listeners will sense your conviction, feed off it, and want to share their belief in you with others. Football immortal Vince Lombardi reportedly said, "If you're not fired with enthusiasm, you'll be fired with enthusiasm!"

Repeat your sound bite at every opportunity. Practice, practice, practice! And always carry a stack of business cards to distribute when making your pitch. If you have brochures or other business materials, distribute those liberally as well.

Networking coach Sarah Michel has four rules for sound bites:

1. Make them catchy but relatable, and eliminate industry buzzwords and abbreviations that don't translate well to others. If someone who has heard your drill just once can repeat it, watch out—you've just created your number one marketing tool and it's free!

2. Establish your expertise up front. Be clear about what you're known for and what differentiates you from others who do what you do.

3. Watch your body language. According to studies, 93 percent of what people pay attention to is not what you say, but how you say it. During your delivery, are you smiling, do you make eye contact? Is your voice, pitch, and rate of speech pleasant?

4. Remember the "three-foot rule." Anyone within three feet of you is a potential network contact. You never know where or when you'll get the opportunity to deliver your powerful introduction. It could be the opportunity of a lifetime!

Work your way around the room, introduce yourself to new faces, and continually give your sound bite. Repetition reinforces name recognition and brand identity, and it builds confidence. Customize your sound bite for different audiences. For example, if you're at an auto dealers' meeting, sprinkle in terms relating to that industry like "on all cylinders," "out of gas," or "cruise control." Using your listeners' language breaks down barriers, lightens the mood, and makes them feel that you're speaking directly to them. In doing so, you become one of them, at least for the time you're together.

You should also prepare a backup sound bite. Be ready to ditch your standard message if it's inappropriate, if someone else in the group has a strikingly similar pitch, or if your sound bite doesn't seem to be going over. Write "ad libs" that you can throw in to sound spontaneous. Remember, your main objective is to get your message across, so if adjusting your sound bite improves your chances, be sure to go for it.

The most important thing to remember is to trust your instincts. You'll quickly learn how and when to alter your message and become adept at making changes based upon your instincts and observations. Work in references to hot news items, scandals, or events that will make your sound bite more relevant, up to date.

Following Through: Further Information

If, after you've given your sound bite, listeners state that they want additional information, give them your brochure, other print materials, or a verbal description. However, if you don't have or don't want to give out print materials, be prepared to verbally describe you, your products, and services. Think of the description as the follow-up or part 2 of your sound bite.

Often it's desirable to simply give your brochure or print materials to those who request more information. It will give them your contact information and allow you to mingle and try to make more connections. However, when you have someone who truly seems interested, it may be worthwhile to spend a bit more time explaining what you do in the hope of building a tighter relationship. Use your instincts.

If listeners do not request additional information, ask if they would like copies of your brochure or print materials. Wait to be asked before delivering a verbal description of you, your products, or services or you could come across as overly pushy and aggressive. Don't volunteer because you could kill off all chances of further contact.

A verbal description can run longer than the ten- to fifteen-second sound bite, but try to keep it between fifteen to thirty seconds. Be considerate of your listeners. They have other things to do, and many have short attention spans or are there to circulate and make contacts, so keep the description of your product or services short. When you finish giving your description, ask if they would like you to send or e-mail them more information.

Think of your description as a mini brochure that explains the benefits you provide. Be specific. Structure your description by listing each benefit that you provide in the order of its importance. List no more than seven benefits, but if your business offers more, as the last item state that you provide additional benefits. Only identify the additional items if asked and then, describe each item in just a few words.

The most common problem with descriptions of yourself, your products, or services is lack of clarity. When you know a subject intimately, it's easy to assume that everyone else understands it. As a result, we tend to use terms specific to our industries and expect others to understand them, which may not be the case.

In describing what you do, be extremely specific. Avoid generalized terms that may create misunderstandings. For example, if you're an accountant, state that you prepare tax returns, appear with clients at IRS audits, and prepare financial statements. Be specific! From this description, people should be able to fully understand what they will be getting from you.

Business Cards

Like your sound bite, your business card is a vital tool in your networking package. Unlike sound bites, business cards should contain all of your contact information so the people you meet can easily get in touch with you. Business cards are reminders: They are intended to jog a contact's memory when he or she comes across your card weeks, months, or even years after you've met. They must provide the information necessary to contact you.

The front of your business card should include:

- Your name and the name of your business
- An explanation of what you do: colonial U.S. furniture dealer, pet portrait photographer, wallpaper hanger. Clarity is essential because contacts may have collected dozens of cards at an event and must be able to ascertain simply by looking at your card precisely what you do.
- The addresses at which you wish to be contacted by postal mail and/or e-mail
- Your telephone, cellular telephone, and/or fax numbers
- Your Web site address

Your card can also include your position or official title, logo, sound bite, motto, or a short slogan. Many people use both sides of their business cards. The backs of cards can provide more information about what you do, testimonials, maps, and other graphic works. Design your card in a style that will reflect the impression you want to convey. Make it distinctive, yet appropriate. Avoid the temptation to clutter your card with so much information that it is difficult to read. If you need space, use both sides, keeping in mind, however, that contacts frequently like to write information on the back of business cards. Before designing your business card, leaf through all the cards that you've collected. Identify features and styles that appeal to you and that you believe will work for you.

The Tools of the Trade

Don't leave home without them—address lists, calendars, and writing materials are the networker's stock in trade. When you make a new contact, few things are as impressive as coming up with a match and immediately giving the new contact all of the match's contact information. And now, the wide availability of personal digital assistants (PDAs), such as Palm Pilots and similar devices as well as cellular telephones, has made carrying this information both easy and fun.

Carrying your calendar with you allows you to arrange appointments on the spot. You can quickly book lunch or make an appointment with a great new contact and avoid the electronic barriers that can make trying to connect so frustrating. Stash pens, pencils, and pads everywhere. Carry them in your pockets, purses, briefcases, glove compartments, and in every room in your home and office. Always be prepared to capture a name, address, or important information.

PDAs and some cellular telephones contain address lists, calendars, and memo applications in one small, tidy package. With these devices, you can instantly beam addresses, contacts, and schedule information to contacts' devices. Some also have digital audio recorders that let you record brief information, such as addresses and phone numbers, for later use.

Backing It Up with Expertise

As we've previously discussed and will discuss further, to build and maintain a successful network you must be an expert. If you want to network with the best, you must be on their level. Expertise must be an integral part of your networking toolkit; you can't get far without it. Even if you can flawlessly deliver a snappy sound bite, have the most compelling description, and the best of all the rest, you still ultimately need expertise. Without expertise you have little of lasting value to give to your network partners. Without expertise you won't be able to contribute, provide benefits, pay your own way, or hold your own and eventually those you want to deal with will no longer want you.

Action Steps

1. Write a killer sound bite that you can deliver in thirty seconds.

   _____

   _____

   _____

   _____

2. Write a killer sound bite that you can deliver in fifteen seconds.

   _____

   _____

   _____

   _____

3. Write a verbal description of your product or service that you can deliver in thirty seconds or less.

   _____

   _____

   _____

   _____

4. List the items to be included on your business card.

   _____

   _____

   _____

   _____

Eight

Approaching the Best Targets

THIS CHAPTER WILL COVER:

Knowing your purpose

Your appearance

Being considerate

Anatomy of a
networking event

Building relationships

Talking business

"Have a bias toward action—let's see
something happen now. You can
break that big plan into small steps
and take the first step right away."

—Richard Thalheimer,
the founder of Sharper Image

It's a steamy, summer Sunday afternoon. You've been working like a dog in the garage cleaning up mountains of junk that you've been stashing and trying to ignore for years. After a few hours, you run out of garbage bags and dash down to the store for a fresh supply.

You find the bags quickly and as you wait to pay, you spot the agent for that fabulous building where you've been dying to move your office. Although you've phoned her dozens of times, she seldom calls back; when she does, it's always too late and the space has been rented. Normally, you would say hello, make small talk, and ask if any vacancies might be coming up. Typically, you would use this chance meeting to turn on the charm and try to talk her into giving you advance notice of upcoming vacancies. But you're sweaty, smelly, and look like a slob. As much as you want to get into that building, you're afraid that your appearance would permanently kill your chances. So you bow your head, turn away, pay for the bags and duck out of the store on the double—letting a golden opportunity pass.

The best networkers are always prepared to network. They know that at any time, at any place, they could meet someone they know or whom they would like to get to know.

Quest for the Best

Workers in the hotel-casino industry face temptation on a daily basis. Many lose their perspective and forget that their companies expect them to get business done and behave professionally. When Neil Mullanaphy was the sales manager at a major Atlantic City hotel-casino, the Hotel and Visitors Authority hired him to be the national sales manager for the opening of its new convention center. Mullanaphy learned that he was selected for his new position because the Authority's top brass had observed him at trade shows, hospitality functions, and other events and noted his ability to network, work the room, and to keep his focus while many of his colleagues strayed. Mullanaphy remained with the Authority for seven years, which gave him the credentials to get his present position as Director of Trade Show and Association Sales at the Mandalay Bay Hotel in Las Vegas.

So whenever they're out, they're always ready, they are never caught unprepared. Savvy networkers never lose sight of their purpose, they know what they want, and they are always neat, well groomed, and appropriately dressed. Successful networkers understand the importance of making the best impression and they always expect and are prepared for the unexpected.

In a similar vein, Rick teaches clients to always watch their language. "Nothing is ever off the record—so NEVER say anything that you wouldn't want to see on the front page of the *New York Times*. I've seen people blow it because they used foul language that offended important people around them. Today, in these permissive times, where it seems like just about anything goes, play it safe. If you don't know the people around you, watch your mouth!"

Know Your Purpose

Whether you go to the store, to the Elks Club, or to the White House, know your purpose. Know why you're there and exactly what you hope to achieve. Never leave anything to chance or wing it; always be ready to give your best. Act appropriately under the circumstances and understand that you never know who is looking at you, watching you, and how that is going to affect you in the future.

Whether you know it or not, people are always watching you. They're monitoring your appearance, demeanor, focus, and resolve. They're making judgments about you, judgments that could affect your life. Know that when you least expect it you will encounter someone or something that can change everything. The next time you go to the movies, be prepared to see that elusive guy who never returns your calls. When you see him, be ready to strut your stuff. When that moment comes, you may decide that it would be inappropriate to pitch him and wiser to just say hello. But be prepared because he just might ask for what you were polite enough to withhold.

Networking Events

Before you attend a networking event:

• *Know your purpose.* Clearly define what you hope to accomplish and set concrete goals. Challenge yourself; don't be satisfied with what you know you can produce, but stretch to accomplish more. (See Jill's goals for networking events in Chapter 4.)

• *Decide how many people you want to meet.* Do you want to find three people who hire speakers, three skateboard experts, or seven ideal prospects for your book club? Identify precisely whom you hope to meet and have a backup list.

- *Set financial goals.* Put precise dollar figures on the business you hope to generate. Tell your projections to friends; it will increase your resolve and help them to spot leads and opportunities for you.
- *Determine what you want to learn.* Clearly identify the areas where you need more knowledge and ask those you meet for their ideas of the best ways to attain it.
- *Have a list of questions.* Think ahead of time about what you could ask other attendees, speakers, or members of the host organization. For example: Why are you here? What are you working on? What books do you recommend? Who are the best people for me to meet?
- *Allow yourself to have fun.* Keep in mind that networking events are not all business; they have a social component. So make it a point to have fun and enjoy yourself. When you are having fun, people will be attracted to you and you will network more successfully.

Business Expertise

As we've previously said, in order to successfully network, you must know your stuff; you must be an expert. You *need* business expertise. Business expertise is not just a one-time accumulation of knowledge that once attained need not be further maintained. To the contrary, business expertise is a continuing process of learning, keeping up, and testing the frontiers, the outer limits of your industry. To do business with the best, you can't merely be up to speed, you must be in the vanguard, among the elite, at the front of the pack.

If you go to an event and can't promptly provide great answers to inquiries about your interests, you're committing networking suicide. You're placing a big black mark next to your name and reputation, which those present will remember and may report to their friends. Overcoming negative impressions is murder because most people won't give you a second chance; they won't waste their time with someone who has already proven unworthy. So, if you're going to network, know your stuff and be able to clearly articulate it. View every question as an opportunity and be ready to make the most of each.

Personal Expertise

Increase your knowledge by getting into the habit of constantly reading. Knowledge is power. Read everything: national and local newspapers, magazines, and a wide variety of books. Read about your business, your interests, and other people's businesses and their interests as well as totally new subjects. Expand your horizons.

Reading places deposits in your knowledge bank and it yields interest that compounds constantly. Hellen Davis, CEO of Indaba Training Specialists, Inc., makes it a point to read the *Wall Street Journal* and *USA Today* in the morning before she attends networking events. Davis feels that having the latest business and national news at her fingertips gives her conversation openings and makes her more interesting, which enhances her ability to make a wide range of contacts that can develop into strong relationships.

Be Considerate

We've all been on the receiving end of bull rushes from relentless pursuers who simply refuse to take no for an answer. These persistent characters have such intense focus, such single-minded insensitivity, that you can't shake them. They seem dauntless, impervious to clear rejections and you have to virtually hit them over the head to ward them off.

In addition, they always catch you at the most inconvenient

or inappropriate times. They deliberately call while you're eating or busy with others. They work weddings, funerals, and social affairs like barracudas swimming in well-stocked waters. Their purpose is to wear you down and it frequently works. Sometimes you buy from or deal with them just to get them off your back, but in most cases, you would rather die than give them a dime. And those who deal with them only do so once because who would want to repeat such unpleasant experiences?

Be considerate of contacts. Don't intrude or overstay your welcome. "People who overtly network or overtly try to sell themselves to others are usually not very successful," Robert Iger, president of the Walt Disney Company, told us. "You have to be ambitious, but you cannot wear ambition on your sleeve. Plus, you cannot 'press' too hard. It's always better to sell yourself with deeds than with blatant salesmanship. Also, you have to wait for the opportunity to present itself and then pounce on it when it comes. People who try to create opportunities look too opportunistic."

Anatomy of a Networking Event

When you go to a networking event, your networking opportunities begin as soon as you get out of the car, the subway, or off the bus. Start conversations with people who enter the building with you, talk to those who are searching for directions or who press the same elevator button. Being pleasant, warm, and friendly never hurts; it doesn't cost a thing, but it can produce huge returns.

When you get to the event, head for the reception table. Sign in and get your nametag and whatever materials are being distributed. If there is a line or there are people gathered by the reception table, begin networking by introducing yourself to those nearby. Start a conversation by finding out who they are and telling them how much you're looking forward to the event. After you've made your first contact, it's usually easier to meet others.

Don't ignore reception desk workers. Often, they are volunteers or key people in the host organization. They may even be the event organizers or hosts. Talking with reception desk workers is networking too; it's extending your contact base and building relationships. So say hello and thank them because they are frequently ignored or treated indifferently. They will appreciate and remember your kindness.

In addition, reception desk workers frequently assist with various chores and can help you throughout the event. They often act as official greeters for the host organizations, and they may know the speakers and experts in attendance. Part of their job may be to make introductions. Don't be afraid to ask greeters or desk workers for help or to introduce you to key people.

Arrive Early

Networking expert Dave Sherman believes that more than 90 percent of those who attend networking events feel uncomfortable to some extent. To overcome your discomfort, he recommends that you arrive at networking events fifteen minutes early. "I know, I know," Sherman states, "only geeks show up early. Not true! I prefer to believe the adage, 'The early bird gets the worm.'" By arriving early, you have the opportunity to meet the people who put on the event before they're inundated with other guests and duties. Usually, they are the movers and shakers of the sponsor organization and are the best folks to connect with, especially if you're new to the organization.

Another reason to show up early is because it's easier to start networking with the five to ten people who are already present than with the fifty to a hundred who will soon arrive. It's hard to walk into a room filled with people and to jump right into your networking mode. When fewer attendees are on hand, you can warm up slowly. Once you break the ice and start talking, it becomes easier and more comfortable to chat with

Quest for the Best

Event organizers know who's who at their events. They also know the movers and shakers as well as the hangers-on who should be avoided. When Hellen Davis, CEO of Indaba Training Systems, Inc., arrives at an event, she finds the promoters or hosts of the event to introduce herself. After explaining who she is, she asks, "If you were me, who would you want to meet?" When they name names, Davis asks them to introduce her. "It's remarkable," she explained, "They (organizers and/or promoters) can interrupt anyone at any time and when they interrupt conversations to introduce me, it elevates my status and makes me seem more important."

others. People you approach often appreciate your interest in them and in turn will become more comfortable and forthcoming with you.

If your nametag isn't preprinted, sign it legibly and print your name in large letters that everyone can read. Some attendees won't be wearing their glasses so help them to identify you by writing your name clearly. Wear your nametag where it can be easily seen.

After putting on their nametags, some people like to step to the side to survey the room before they venture further. Jill always locates the food area because it's an excellent place to socialize. Sooner or later, everyone at events wanders over to the food area where the atmosphere is more relaxed. As you walk toward the food area, look for opportunities to network.

People like to hang around food areas. It gives them a break and the presence of food loosens them up. Around food, most people tend to be more open and at ease. Since the atmosphere around the food isn't as charged, it's easier to strike up conversations with openings such as, "Isn't the Danish great?" "Oh, those egg rolls look good," or "Oh well, I know I shouldn't, but . . . "

Read Those Nametags

At events sponsored by Executive Moms, a New York City organization for women who balance their careers as business executives with being mothers, attendees wear two nametags. One nametag has the woman's name and where she resides while the other lists the names and ages of her children. The two nametags increase the opportunities for the women at the events to talk, interact, and build relationships, according to Marisa Thalberg, Executive Moms' founder and president.

Rosters and Programs

If the sponsor provides a roster of attendees, check the names listed to identify whom you would like to meet and whom you know. Most rosters are handed out when you sign in, so study them as soon as you get the chance. If you can, obtain and read the roster in advance. Some rosters provide information about the attendees and it's surprising how much of it will come to mind when you meet that person face-to-face. When you go to trade shows and large conferences, get a list of attendees and exhibitors beforehand as well as the schedule of when you can attend the exhibits.

Save all advertisements or solicitations that describe the program. Note who will be speaking, leading workshops, or presenting awards. Find out as much as you can about them. At the event, ask others in attendance what they know about the speakers, if they've read their books or taken their courses. If you are undecided about which workshop to attend, ask others.

Scan the main areas to see where everyone congregates. Discover whether they are moving around or standing in groups and where the energy is. If people all gather at a certain place, try to discover what is going on. Move in the direction of the people and the energy. If you see someone alone, introduce yourself and begin to network.

Greet and be cordial to the people you know, but concentrate on meeting new people. If you want to make new contacts, don't sit or hang out with friends or business associates, but seek out new faces and get to meet them.

Jill Lublin advises people to "act like a butterfly." When you meet friends at events, it is not the appropriate time to involve yourselves in prolonged discussions that go into the intimate details of their lives. It's the time to network, to get down to business. When Jill sees someone she knows at a networking event, she simply says hello and asks how he or she is without getting into a deep conversation. Then she moves on. With people she doesn't know, Jill invests more time. Jill believes that networking events are primarily to meet new people. Although she loves the social aspects of seeing old friends, Jill understands that the purpose of networking events is to make new contacts.

If Jill knows two people in a group of three, she will say hello to the two she knows and introduce herself to the person she doesn't know. At networking events, Jill always speaks and introduces herself first because attendees may be uncomfortable introducing themselves, or even freeze up.

Approaching Others

Approach people when your eyes meet or they smile at you and hold their smile. Try to connect with people who communicate with vibrancy and enthusiasm and seem interested and excited. Look for energy and vitality.

Before approaching others, look for body language that reveals if they are open to talking or not interested. Those with their arms crossed over their torso, who are unsmiling, looking around nervously or who step back when you approach are not

open. People who are not into talking with you won't acknowledge you or will acknowledge you briefly, unsmilingly, and then
quickly turn or step away. Frequently, they'll give you a quick,
sharp nod. They're sending out "Do not approach" signals. Do
what they ask, and leave them alone! If they don't want to talk,
simply smile pleasantly and move on.

People who are open to talking to you will usually smile,
nod, make an opening comment, or introduce themselves. Look
at their eyes: If they hold your gaze or don't seem to look straight
through you, continue your approach. Open people hug, laugh,
smile, look people straight in the eyes, and lean forward toward
the person they're talking with.

Jill likes to approach people when they're standing alone
because it usually means that they don't know what to do next.
Although she doesn't spend a lot of time with them, she tries to
make them comfortable. Jill will also escort them over to groups
that she feels she can enter and be a part of.

When people are in a group, read the looks and gestures of
the group members to determine if you're welcome. If members
of a group acknowledge you or smile or nod to you, smile or
nod back. Introduce yourself only if it doesn't interrupt the conversation and even then, be brief. Give your sound bite. If you
feel that you're not welcome in their conversation, simply smile
and slip away.

When you approach a group that is involved in conversation:

- Remain silent until you can figure out what they are
  discussing.
- Listen and remain silent until you have something that is
  both relevant and of value to add; otherwise don't speak.
- Remember that irrelevant and/or valueless comments are
  rude interruptions that most people resent.

Often, it pays to position yourself to the side of a group
where you can eavesdrop on their conversation. After listening

for a while, you may find that you're not interested in talking with them. In addition, you could learn something that would ease your entry into the group or that would smoothe your approach when you subsequently come across group members during the event.

When someone you would like to meet is surrounded and it's hard to approach, don't be intimidated. Be patient and wait your turn because most people are usually approachable; you just may have to wait. Speakers or celebrities at events can be hard to reach. If, after patiently waiting, you still have not gotten your chance, see if the speakers have "guards" or people escorting them. If so, tell their escorts, "I'd love to speak with Jane; when is the best time to contact her?" Sometimes the escorts will tell you, "Just wait here," and will stand with you in such a way that the speaker will notice and give you your chance.

Card Shuffling

When Jill attends networking events, she wears outfits with two side pockets. In her right pocket, she keeps her business cards, which she liberally hands out. In her left pocket, she puts the business cards she receives from others. On the rare occasion when she wears an outfit that doesn't have two side pockets, she carries a compartmentalized holder that has separate sections for her book, business cards, postcards, marketing materials, and other people's cards.

When Jill receives other people's business cards, she writes notes on their cards before putting them in her pocket or holder, even if they are still present. Jill feels that most people are flattered that she is interested and organized enough to note information about them on the back of their card. However, if you feel uncomfortable, say something like, "Let me write this down so I won't forget."

Jill doesn't believe in preplanning opening gambits because she considers them insincere and transparent. "People sense and resent insincerity, they know it's manipulative, and it turns them off." Instead, Jill gives her sound bite, relies on her instincts, and opens by complimenting a pretty outfit (only when she means it) or commenting on something she observed. The only thing Jill preplans, she stresses, is what she says about her business. Nothing else is planned.

When you meet people try hard to remember their names. To improve your ability to remember names, see Chapter 12. Repeat contacts' names: Find ways to work them into conversations and call them by name when you speak and subsequently see them. Look for opportunities to give genuine compliments. Compliments are great icebreakers, especially those that are astute. However, don't give compliments when you don't mean them or the word will soon circulate and your believability quotient will crash. Tell contacts when you enjoyed what they said, agreed with what they wrote, admired what they did, or even liked what they wore.

Leaving a Group

People who enter a group don't have to stay in the conversation. You can excuse yourself at any time, but prepare an exit strategy. Before the event, think of basic lines that will let you politely slip out of a conversation without appearing to be rude. For example, you smile and simply say, "I need to get a drink," "I need to say hello to someone," or "Oh, I need to coordinate my ride home" and then walk away. And, no matter how badly you want to leave the group, never be discourteous or overly abrupt.

Unlike most people in the world, we Americans aren't taught to separate social and business situations. As a result, in the United States, business talk is always considered appropriate, which in certain situations can cause problems. For example, in social situations, it's polite to remain in conversations that no longer involve you and leaving the conversation could be considered rude. On the other hand, in business situations, staying in conversations that no longer involve you is rude.

At networking events, when a new person enters the conversation and the subject changes so that it no longer concerns or is about you, move on. By remaining in the conversation, you can dampen the dynamic, sap the energy, and inhibit the creation of new and meaningful dialogs. When it no longer involves you, politely say goodbye and leave. If you want to make a specific plan, say, "It's been great talking to you, should I call you next week; what day would be good?" And then leave. If you don't want any further contact, say, "It was nice seeing you. I'll look forward to seeing you at the next event."

Many people find networking events uncomfortable and don't know how to act. Try to be kind, understanding, and compassionate, but remember your purpose. Excusing yourself from unproductive conversations may be uncomfortable, but it is necessary. At networking events, you're there for business, not to socialize or to nurse uncomfortable people.

Building Relationships

Networking and relationship building, like most good things, don't happen instantly, but take time. They must be developed in stages, nurtured, step by step, with patience, care, and persistence. Relationship building starts the moment you see a target, even before you say a word or stick out your hand and say hello. When you approach targets, your primary purpose is to make contacts with the best people that can bloom into strong relationships, not to sell your product or service.

Never underestimate the impact of a first impression and how long it lasts. People long remember initial contacts and those impressions affect the manner in which they deal with you.

So make a strong initial impression. Stand tall, smile, look directly at your target, and offer your hand. Don't try to bowl him or her over, just try to connect. Approach targets with the intention of getting to know them and building friendships and solid relationships. When you meet and get to know people, think what you can do for them and with whom you can match them.

Be selective in choosing your targets because you only have limited time and resources. Develop your instincts to hone in on targets with the best potential and avoid those who only want to take from you. These people have few good contacts and only want access to your network partners.

A System for Avoiding Rejection

Business expert Mitch Axelrod has developed a system that he calls "Rejection-Proof Networking." In 1982, when Mitch was a financial planner, he wanted million-dollar clients. So he developed a five-step approach that he called "Take a Millionaire to Lunch." Using this approach, he increased his income 600 percent in two years—from $16,000 in 1982 to $100,000 in 1984. From 1990 to 1995, he used his method again in a different business and increased his fees by tenfold.

Mitch's approach is:

1. *List your twenty best centers of influence!*
List the names of the twenty people you know who could help you most. Don't prejudge, prequalify, or predetermine if they will help you. Aim high! You can also make a second list of the wealthiest people you know.

2. *Categorize each person as an A, B, or C resource.*
A = Absolutely can help
B = Better than 50/50 chance
C = Might help, but maybe not!

3. *Send a letter to or call your A List.*

Ask them to meet you in person for fifteen minutes. Tell them, "I value your opinion. I trust you to tell me the truth. I'd like your advice, counsel, and help." Be genuine, sincere, and really mean it! Don't even think about trying to sell them anything. You want their advice and help. Period! Their help will be worth a small fortune to you.

4. *When you meet them, explain What—Why—Who—How—Where.*

What—you are doing and what your goals are. Be clear about what you want and where you want to go.

Why—you decided to do what you're doing. Demonstrate your passion and commitment.

Who—you are looking to reach. Make a list of the type of people who would be in the best position to further your quest and give you access to their resources and relationships.

How—you want help. Describe the resources, relationships, and results you are looking for. Be as detailed as you can.

Where—should I go next? Where can you send me to get what I'm looking for?

5. *Now, ask one or all of these BIG questions:*
"What would you do if you were me?"
"What advice would you give your best friend?"
"How would you handle this situation?"
"Who can I talk to—where should I go from here?"

It's crucial to keep in mind that most people want to help. If you're courageous and determined enough to ask, you will find the help you need. When people are approached to sign up for or buy into something, they often get defensive and put up their guard. If they don't buy the product or service, they may find it awkward to recommend it or the person who offered it. Their sales resistance will make it harder for them to be a networking resource for you.

When making a request of a contact, be direct and specific. State what you need clearly and descriptively. Be honest and up front about what you want and don't be greedy. Be grateful for every effort made in your behalf.

Talking Business

After you develop a relationship with a contact, don't talk business or ask for a favor until you're absolutely certain that your contact will be receptive. If you feel that asking for help would kill the relationship, back off and live to fight another day. Ideally, by the time you ask for help, you will have given your new contact leads or connected him or her with your network partners.

When you're ready:

- Be direct and totally honest.
- Explain precisely what you need.
- State exactly how your contact can help.
- Inquire if your contact knows others who might help.
- Point out what you have to offer.
- Stress the importance of your contact's help.
- If your contact gives you a lead, request permission to use his or her name.
- Ask how you can repay or help your contact.
- Express your gratitude for your contact's help.

Most contacts are realists who understand the reciprocal nature of business. If they like you, owe you, or better yet, if they believe in you, they'll be happy to recommend you. It's good business and if you do well, it will make them look good. When you approach contacts:

- Try to get three leads. Expect your contacts to be cautious until they're convinced that you consistently deliver high-quality work.
- Be patient and persistent.
- Ask for the chance to prove yourself.
- Take less, or nothing at all, to get your foot in the door.

Referral Fees

In some business situations, you should clarify in advance whether your contacts expect referral fees. If they do, clarify exactly how much they want. Quantify the amount or percentage they expect and make sure that you are both in full agreement. In some businesses and localities, referral fees are unethical. Since the rules vary from place to place, check out what's acceptable where you transact that business.

When you get business via a referral, find ways to show your appreciation if your contact can't or won't accept a referral fee. Consider giving a gift, tickets to an event, or a charitable contribution; or perform extra or personal work for them to say thanks. Gestures of gratitude are greatly appreciated and are good business.

Action Steps

1. Write three icebreakers to start a conversation with a stranger.

_____

_____

_____

2. Write three exit lines to leave a conversation that is no longer productive.

_____

_____

_____

3. List the names of twenty people you know who could help you the most.

_____

_____

_____

_____

_____

_____

_____

_____

_____

4. Compose a short letter asking someone on your list to meet you for fifteen minutes.

_____

_____

_____

_____

Nine

Turning Contacts into Partners

THIS CHAPTER WILL COVER:

Utilizing a system

Prioritizing

Making your move

Saying thanks

Negative responses

How to follow up

"You can be the master of working a room and leave each networking event with a pocketful of business cards, but if you do not follow up with these people and others already in your network, you will never be successful at networking."

—Andrea Nierenberg, author of
Nonstop Networking

After you've made an interesting new contact whom you would like to know better, and who could help your career or other aspects of your life, how do you capitalize on that contact and make that person a member of your network? The answer is by following up. All of the work that you've done to make and impress contacts will be lost if you don't systematically follow up.

Let's hope that when you met your new contact, you followed our suggestions and rattled off that killer sound bite. Hopefully, it impressed your contact and elicited further interest. If it did, did you chat and exchange business cards or contact information? Did you make a date or clearly state that you would like to get together or keep in touch? If you did, great! That's a start, but it's only a start; it's just the tip of the iceberg.

When you make new contacts, you're just getting your foot in the door. Once you have that initial opening, the object is to get in deeper, to get past the gatekeeper and move all the way to the Oval Office. For some people, making initial contacts comes easy; it's an instinctive part of their nature. In most cases, these contacts are brief, little more than introductions that don't go further. However, on occasion, you will want to turn first encounters into more solid relationships, which takes far more time and effort. The bulk of what it takes is following up.

For many, following up is uncomfortable. They usually find

it uncomfortable because they don't know what to do. Few of us have ever been taught to network and for many it doesn't come naturally—at least, that's what we feel. Ironically, when most of us were kids, it was easy to enter into new relationships. We would meet a new kid and see him or her the next day at school, at Little League, or at dance class. If we had to call a new kid, it got a little stickier, but generally it was no big deal because most everybody was eager to make new friends. But when we became adults, everything changed.

Most adults find it hard to follow up. Some are shy, are afraid to be a nuisance, or appear to be groveling. The majority, however, simply feel awkward and ill at ease. To them it's unnatural. They see networking as selling and although all of us sell something, they don't want to be perceived as salespersons. Well, if you feel that way, get over it because it's probably holding you back.

Following up promptly isn't just good business, it's smart business. Following up is as important as any other business task, but most people don't approach it systematically. They think that it should be easy, and they justify not following up because they are so busy or it's not their style. As a result, they follow up only when they can steal time from other tasks that they consider more important or in desperate attempts to breathe new life into waning efforts.

When you first try to follow up, it may feel strange; it may even feel unpleasant, but you'll soon adjust to it. It won't take long, but it will take some time and work and it helps to have a plan. The big surprise is that following up can be fun and it can produce rewards beyond your expectations. It can enable you to meet and form relationships with wonderful people who become close friends and enrich your life.

Create a System

First of all, you really must save business cards, contact information, and other contact literature. Treat them like receipts that you might need for an IRS audit. Keep all of the original information you collect in a designated place and hold on to it even after you have entered all of the contact information in your files.

Develop a system and religiously follow up in a businesslike manner. After making a contact, don't just go home and toss your contact's business card in with the pile of others you collected over the last six months. Business cards won't follow up by themselves. They won't go to the phone, call contacts, and make dates for lunch. But you should if you're serious about networking!

Buy or create a system to prioritize and file contact information. Use your Palm Pilot or any of the excellent contact-management software on the market. Contact-management programs are readily available and most are easy to set up and use. Or create your own system. Whatever you choose should contain room for your contact's:

- Name
- Business/employer
- Street address
- E-mail address
- Telephone number
- Fax number

- Backup telephone numbers including cellular phone numbers
- Web site address
- Specialty area
- Family information

Also record:

- The names of common friends or contacts
- Source information on how and where you got your contact's name
- Background and personal information such as your contact's education, interests, accomplishments, awards, likes, dislikes, political affiliations, religious affiliations, charitable work, and stories or jokes he or she told
- Dates you last spoke and what was said
- Your next step
- Future plans or actions

Learning to Prioritize

Ideally, it's best to enter contact information in your files as close to the initial meeting as possible. Record it that evening or the first thing the next day. Then communicate with your contact via e-mail or postal mail within two or three days to follow up. Unfortunately, most mere mortals are not that organized, disciplined, or efficient. We tend to throw all the contact information we collect into a heap and get to it when we get to it—which won't do! If you've collected a bunch of business cards, prioritize them to determine whom you want to call first. Then enter the contact information into your system. Move first to communicate with:

1. Those you promised to call or e-mail. Place the business cards for those you agreed to contact in a separate stack. Then enter their contact information in your files. Make sure to e-mail or call them within the two or three days of your initial contact. By communicating promptly, you demonstrate that you are a person of your word who does what he or she promised and is a person of action. Following up promptly also allows you to build upon the warmth or excitement generated by your exchange or the spirit and fond memories of the event.

2. Contacts who could be important to you. Record his or her contact information in your files immediately. Communicate with him or her within a few days, but no later than a week after you met. Most people are flattered when you call them promptly, especially if the initial contact was strong. If you made a good connection, contacts will usually be delighted to hear from you and be eager to pick up where you left off. Calling promptly will not make you seem desperate or uncool. Besides, it's childish and self-defeating to try to be cool with people who could matter.

Call soon. After a week or two, memories get buried by the demands of fast-paced, busy lives—even when you made the most terrific impression. After two or more weeks, consider your-self lucky to be remembered at all.

Classify the business cards you collect in three categories, the:

- *A List*—Those whom you promised to call and most want to court. Also include those you should thank.
- *B List*—Contacts you would like to spend time with again or help, but not immediately.
- *C List*—People on whose radar screen you wish to remain, but with whom you don't want to meet at this time.

Separate your A List into those contacts whom you can help. Focus first on those you can help in order to form the habit of making giving your first priority. By giving first, you build goodwill and give your contacts a strong reason to remember you and want to reciprocate. As Mike Litman said, "Leaders go first." So make the first move; don't wait for them to communicate with you.

Call or e-mail your contact within a week of your introduc-tion to offer your help. Strike while the memory of your intro-duction is still fresh. Most people will feel flattered by your quick response. If you wait over two weeks, they won't remember you as well and you will essentially be making a cold call.

Make Your Move

Plan your strategy. Decide whom to communicate with first. Do you want to call a first generation contact who can deliver pre-cisely what you need? Or would it be better to proceed incre-mentally, building step by step until you can reach a target who can provide what you want? Usually, the best and easiest approach is to be straightforward. Send a handwritten note or an e-mail similar to the following example:

Hi Bill-

It was great meeting you at the Chamber mixer. Every time I think about that story you told about Frank, I crack up laughing. Attached is an article on new monitors that might interest you.

Are you free for lunch this Thursday, March 21st? Hope you can make it because it would be fun.

My best to Phil.

Rick

In your follow-up communiqué, state where you met and include a reference that will make the connection closer and more personal such as the reference to the story about Frank above. Attach or send articles, cartoons, or information that might interest your contact and open up subjects for future communications. Make sure that whatever you send or attach is relevant; otherwise you'll be sending irritating spam. In your message, refer to shared experiences or special events that have occurred.

State your request directly and specifically. If you merely say, "Let's get together for lunch," without suggesting a particular date, it may never happen. By being specific, you shift the responsibility to your contact to either accept or decline and you keep the flow of communication alive.

If you are looking for information, be clear about what you want. State, "When we met at the NSA conference, you mentioned that you have a friend who works for Steven Spielberg and that he might be interested in my screenplay. Can I e-mail him and use your name? If so, please send me his e-mail address." Follow Rick's example by asking those you e-mail how you can help. Frequently, the question will not be appropriate, but when it is, try to work it in.

The immediacy of e-mail makes it ideal for following up. Instead of being transported for days, like a letter or note, e-mail is instantaneous . . . it's the people sending and responding to e-mail who take longer. Through e-mail you can quickly set up follow-up appointments or meetings. Notes or letters may be more personal and more appropriate for specific contacts, but e-mail quickly gets the job done and in most cases is perfectly acceptable.

Follow-up phone calls are as fast as e-mail, but busy people are harder to reach by phone. Unlike telephone messages, most e-mails are usually read and responded to promptly. When you're trying to reach the top people, send items that will attract their attention. In addition to sending informative articles, you can send joke or gag gifts, but don't be a pest. Select what you send judiciously, and be sure that it's relevant or will interest them. Don't relentlessly inundate your contact with unrequested information or your subsequent communications won't even be opened.

After you send articles or announcements, telephone your

Follow Up on Your Follow-Up

Professional speaker and marketing consultant Ken Glickman recommends a method of following up that will create a great impression. When you come across an item that could help a contact, don't immediately fax or e-mail it. Instead, first send an e-mail saying, "I found something very useful and I'm going to send it to you Wednesday." When it arrives on Wednesday, you've accomplished two objectives:

1. Helping your contact by sending something he or she might find valuable

2. Demonstrating that you are a person who does as he or she promised

With this approach, you can subtly create an excellent impression. However, the item you send must be special; anything less will relegate you to the pack with all of the others trying to attract your contact's attention.

contacts. Ask what they think about the item you sent, how it could impact them, and ask them to explain it to you from their perspective. Show interest and concern, but don't try to sell them. Simply try to create a positive impression and build for the future. If you can't get through by phone, do it via e-mail.

When you hear about developments related to your contacts, call and ask how it will affect them. Show interest and concern. Again, don't try to sell; simply try to be a friend. When appropriate, ask how you can help.

Always Say "Thanks"

Whenever someone introduces you, recommends you, endorses you, speaks well of you, or helps you in any way, quickly and clearly express your gratitude. Say thanks while you are still enthusiastic and can fully communicate the depths of your feelings. Thank everyone who has been kind, warm, and pleasant, or done a good job. Express your appreciation on the spot and let them know how much their assistance means to you.

People remember your gratitude; it makes them feel happy that they helped you. When you boil it down, thanking others is recognizing and acknowledging their efforts and, unfortunately, it isn't expressed often enough. Expressing thanks costs absolutely nothing and takes just seconds to state, but it provides a great way to make others happy. And, as a result, they will usually remember and think fondly of you. When you make those who help you feel pleased, they will usually make even greater efforts to assist you again.

Expressing your appreciation is an important part of following up. It opens the door for closer, warmer, and frequently more productive interactions. It's an important habit to form and provides a wonderful example for people to observe.

The best, most personal way to show your appreciation is by writing a handwritten note; it makes the strongest impression. It

Quest for the Best

In August 2002, marketing strategist Robyn Levin attended a networking event in Dallas with 500 other women business owners/entrepreneurs. The event was hosted by eWomenNetwork. Robyn was so impressed with the event that when it was over, she made a point of personally thanking and congratulating Sandra and Kym Yancy, the founders of eWomenNetwork.

Two months later, Robyn was scheduled to attend a wedding in Dallas, so she called Kym to see if they could meet. As a marketing strategist, Robyn is always looking for opportunities to develop strategic alliances to promote products and services for clients and herself. At their meeting, Robyn updated Kym on her ideas to create opportunities for eWomen members and they explored joint marketing ideas including her eBook, *Capsules: Top 25 Tips & Creative Remedies for Women and Small Business Owners.* Over the next few months, Robyn and Kym kept in touch and before long, she invited her to be the eWomenNetwork's West Coast Corporate Alliance Representative, which Robyn happily accepted.

doesn't have to be elaborate or on fancy or expensive stationery. Simply expressing your gratitude on a nice note or postcard will do fine. People remember and are impressed by and touched when you take time from your busy life to thank them. Have you ever received a handwritten thank-you note from a powerful person? It makes you feel wonderful, exhilarated, and as if you were ten feet tall. It's a wonderful touch that you never forget!

Phone calls can also be effective and personal. They allow you to articulate the full extent of your gratitude and can extend into warm, pleasant, and fun-filled exchanges. However, phone calls can run on and it can be hard to cut them off without sounding curt. E-mail is less personal than notes and phone calls, but is quick. If well-written, e-mail can be just as expressive as notes and phone calls. Often, it's better to send a quick, thank-you e-mail than to wait and send the perfect handwritten note. Remember, the method you choose for saying thanks is secondary to saying it promptly.

To express your thanks for special favors, think about sending a gift. Even standards like flowers, candy, or wine are greatly appreciated, especially when they were not expected. A small gift is a wonderful way to say thanks and be fondly remembered. Be generous in thanking others. Develop the reputation for giving more than is necessary, especially of your time and efforts.

Negative Responses

If your contact isn't responsive, try to preserve the connection. The top people are usually busy and may not have the time to respond to you now. However, things always change and today's rejections could be tomorrow's acceptances so don't abandon the contact. Be patient, but persistent. Gently remind your contact about yourself without being a pain.

Send reminders like articles or information that might interest your contact and include brief notes that say, "I thought this might interest you. Hope all is well. My best. Phil." Don't overdo it or you will be considered a pest and your communiqués

Watch Your Language
E-mail can read more harshly than intended. So take great pains to word your e-mails in soft language. To avoid harshness, some folks send their e-mail to themselves first. They read them and then, if they set the proper tone, they forward them to the intended recipient . . . but only after they read them first.

will be avoided. Send only truly relevant information and set extremely high standards for what you send.

If you get an outright rejection, ask, "Who else can you recommend that I call?" If you receive a name or names, obtain permission to use your contact's name. If he or she agrees, call and say, "Don Martin of the *Times* suggested that I call you."

Remember to keep your contacts in the loop. Report on how your dealings with his or her referrals went and clearly express your thanks. Report back whenever you reach a major plateau.

If you do finalize a deal through your contact's referral, send a gift to show your appreciation. You don't have to break the bank or buy a lavish gift, but send something, even a plant, flowers, or candy.

In following up, a delicate balance must be maintained between persistence and pushiness. Although you frequently have to be persistent, be persistent with a light and gentle touch. When you e-mail or call contacts, be warm, friendly, fun, and grateful. Don't be pushy, overly forceful, or aggressive. Approach contacts with soft, little nudges, not nuclear warheads. Be patient because if you're too pushy, they may give you the boot to get you off their backs, which is the last thing that you want.

An Essential Strategy

Following up is not simply a short-term strategy; it's a critical discipline that is essential in networking. Following up is how you convert leads into lasting network relationships. It's a time-tested method that is critical in building and maintaining productive networks. Following up broadens your contact base, and it also sharpens your skills and impresses others by demonstrating your professionalism, reliability, and dedication.

How to Follow Up

Schedule a regular time each day to follow up, such as each morning when you get to work. Schedule it like an appointment and enter it on your calendar. Allot a set amount of time to enter contact information and call or e-mail contacts.

In e-mail, summarize the reason you are communicating in the subject line. For example, "Lunch on June 6th." Then elaborate on it more fully in the body of the e-mail message. This way, your contacts can know the purpose of your communiqué without having to open it and can deal with it at a convenient time. Keep e-mails short. Say just enough to clearly make your point.

If you leave a telephone message, first state your name and then say why you are calling. It will provide context for who you are and the reason you are calling. If you call and reach your contact, state your name, ask how he or she is, and then say why you called.

For e-mail correspondence, send e-mail with a return receipt in order to verify that it was received. Also program your e-mail to automatically provide your contact information in a signature file. In addition to your name, business, address, telephone number, fax number, and Web address, signature files can also give your business motto or your sound bite. When sending faxes, include a cover sheet that provides the same.

When a contact shows interest and promises to call you back, try to pin him or her down regarding when you can expect the call. If he or she doesn't call within the appointed time, which is likely, call or e-mail to provide him or her with a gentle reminder.

No matter what you do, there will be times when you are not the right fit for certain contacts. On those occasions, try to salvage something positive by being pleasant and keeping the channels of communication open. If you can't build a business relationship, try to build a friendly relationship. Thank contacts for their time and request the names of others who might help, as well as your contacts' permission to say they referred you.

Follow-Up Log

Record your follow-up efforts in a log that you can quickly access. Record in the log the date and time of each follow-up attempt, who you contacted, the type of contact (E = e-mail, T = telephone, L = letter, FTF = face-to-face meeting, etc.), the subject of the contact, and the outcome or result. The outcome could be "reached answering machine" or "spoke with Debbie Levick and scheduled lunch for April 5th."

Sample Follow-Up Log

Date/Time	Contact	Subject	Type	Outcome
2/11/04 – 9 A.M.	Ed Galvez, Producer	Marfa Trip	E	N/R. Follow up next week
2/11/04 – 9:30 A.M.	Kate Slavin	New ads	T	Spoke, showed interest
2/12/04 – 1 P.M.	Jeff Long, Studio	Marfa trip	E	N/R. Follow up on 2/19
2/14/04 – 1:30 P.M.	Weinberg Bros.	Lakers tickets	T	Spoke, will send
2/14/04 – 2 P.M.	Leslie Fleming	Wedding	E	Will meet on 2/17

It Will Get Easier!

Believe it or not, with practice, following up gets easier; it even gets to be routine and second nature. As you become more proficient, you'll find that important contacts respect professionalism and prefer to deal with professionals because they know that they can usually rely upon them. So when you follow up in a well-planned, disciplined, and timely fashion, important contacts might be more willing to deal with you.

Benefits from following up also spill over to other facets of your life. They teach you patience, understanding, and diplomacy. They give you a better idea how to plan, position yourself, wait your turn, and seize opportunities. Following up isn't just persistence, although you must be persistent, it's being considerate, respectful, and wise. It's treating people as you wish to be treated—just like networking.

On occasions, you'll get lucky. Everybody will ask you to lunch, invite you to his or her club, and introduce you to the A List members. On these lucky streaks, nothing will go wrong and you will be the toast of the town, the "flavor of the month," the person most in demand, with whom everyone wants to be associated. Treat those times with reverence by appreciating your good fortune and realizing that it's probably just a temporary phenomenon. When you're on top, leverage your success by treating everyone well. Be kind, understanding, gracious, and generous. Help whomever needs help—whether or not they ask, look for opportunities to help. Apply your good fortune, your moment in the sun, to give generously to others.

The Rule of Seven

Rick teaches his employees that "the Rule of Seven" applies to following up. According to the rule, it takes seven steps, calls, or e-mails, to actually get a booking. "Expect six no's before you get a yes—or, after seven attempts, you may never get a yes and have to move on. Whenever someone says no, be gracious. A no may be no for now, but not forever. Never burn bridges," Rick advises.

When you're following up, it may not take seven calls or e-mails to connect with your contact; he or she may cut you off after just one. Nevertheless, be prepared to make seven honest attempts. If, after giving it seven wholehearted tries, you haven't connected, move on. Rethink your options and go to Plan B. Move that contact to your C List. Drop him or her an occasional e-mail or postal mailing to remain on his or her radar screen, but bypass him or her and get on with your life.

Although your contact may not need or want to see you now, be professional. Proceed with dignity and respect for your contact's time. Networking is a long-term process, not just quick hit-or-miss shots. It's about how you live your life and how you treat others. By being understanding, patient, and principled, doors will remain open for you and sometime in the future you could connect.

When you receive rejections, or when contacts don't respond favorably, don't become discouraged or upset. Don't get angry or give up. Instead, turn to other sources, focus your energy on other contacts, and keep on plugging! Building and maintaining relationships involves following up, following up, following up—but it can get you the pot of gold.

Advocates and Strategic Alliance Lists

Try this exercise: List the top twenty-five individuals who provide you with business and who are members of your inner circle. Business advisor Mark LeBlanc calls this your advocate's list because the people on this list will really go to bat for you; they're your prime supporters. Advocates won't just call their contacts to recommend you, they will call and set up meetings or try to convince their contacts that they can't live or stay in business without hiring you or using your products or services.

In addition to her advocates' list, Jill also maintains a strategic alliance list. On this list, she includes people who do not necessarily send her business, but with whom she wants to keep in touch. Fill this list with the most outstanding people. "You meet and spend time with remarkable people. And then life and all the millions of things we have to do interrupts and you lose touch. My strategic alliance list lets me keep in touch," Jill says. Since Jill is a professional speaker, she also maintains a list of bureaus and organizations that book professional speakers.

Every month, send the twenty-five members on your advocates list something that will remind them about you, LeBlanc advises. It doesn't have to be elaborate or expensive, just enough to make the recipients think positively of you. For example, you can send a simple e-mail greeting, a newsletter, an article, a cartoon, statistical information, or a discount for using your product or service. Constantly look for interesting and fun items that you can send to your advocates.

Every month, Jill sends something to those on her speakers' bureau list. One month she may send them her speaker's sheet, a single page that describes the content of her presentations. On other months, she may send her media sheet, which is the most up-to-date listing of her media exposures, tapes of her presentations, or excerpts of articles mentioning or quoting her.

Jill sends material to those on her strategic alliance list every three months. Often she sends the same items that went to speakers' bureaus, but on other occasions she will send something more personal. The purpose of these contacts is primarily to keep her "on top of their mind."

At least once each year, contact everyone listed in your database. Send letters for special occasions such as Christmas, the New Year, birthdays, anniversaries, Thanksgiving, tax time, your favorite hero's birthday—or just invent some other reason. Let them know that you're still around, still in business, and that you're thinking of them.

When you contact the members of your advocates' list or database via postal mail, score extra points by personalizing your communications with the addition of a short, handwritten note or comment. Taking the time and making the effort to add, "Hope all is well!", "Miss seeing you!", or "How about lunch soon?" will go a long way to rekindling and maintaining important relationships.

Both Jill and Rick also use e-zines, e-mail newsletters, to stay in the forefront of their clients' and contacts' minds. Every month, their firms, Promising Promotion and Planned Television Arts, send out tips and solid factual information, which is also posted on their Web sites (*www.promisingpromotion.com* and *www.plannedtvarts.com*). In fact, PTA's e-zine is called "The Tip Sheet." Since the information supplied is factual, it can help recipients and is not viewed as simply a self-serving promotion.

Action Steps

1. Identify four contact management systems or software programs to investigate for your use.

   _____

   _____

   _____

   _____

2. Set forth the criteria for contacts to be included on your A List.

   _____

   _____

   _____

   _____

3. Compose a standard thank-you note that you could adapt for contacts to send or e-mail your appreciation.

   _____

   _____

   _____

   _____

4. List three ways that you can follow up with contacts who do not respond to your approaches.

   _____

   _____

   _____

Ten

Organized Networking Groups

THIS CHAPTER WILL COVER:

Types of networking groups

Network Associates

Circles of Eight

The Hubbel Group

AmSpirit Business Connections

eWomenNetwork

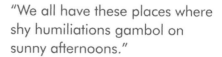

"We all have these places where shy humiliations gambol on sunny afternoons."

—W. H. Auden, poet

Whenever people congregate, networking opportunities exist. Therefore, most good networkers join groups where they can make new contacts and incorporate them into their networks. Groups are ideal for networking because they bring together like-minded individuals who frequently share common backgrounds, interests, and goals. Through groups, networkers can expand their reach and make connections with those it might otherwise take them considerably longer to meet.

Many of the groups where people now network were not organized to facilitate networking. Usually, these groups were started to promote business, social, community, religious, charitable, or other endeavors. Such groups can be trade associations, your Wednesday night card game, or your bowling team as well as business, social, religious, community, and charitable and service organizations. They also can include youth and recreational groups, athletic teams, fraternities and sororities, and alumni organizations.

Although trade and industry associations were not founded as networking organizations, they have evolved into unparalleled networking facilitators. Trade association events draw the top people in the industry because they provide them with a forum where they can shine among their peers. At these events you can identify the major players and the up-and-comers and learn about the pressing issues of concern. Savvy networkers become involved in trade association activities because they can meet, interact, and work with the best people in their field.

In addition to trade associations, other major networking organizations include business organizations such as Chambers of Commerce; IBI Global, Inc.; Consulting Alliance (the Entrepreneurial Edge); and Shared Vision Network. Service organizations—which include the Masons, Kiwanis, Elks, Lions, and Rotary Clubs, and Soroptimists—also provide outstanding venues for networking.

Recently, groups have been popping up everywhere that exist primarily to help their members network. We call these "organized networking groups" or "network-focused groups." Large network-focused groups include national organizations such as eWomenNetwork; LeTip International, Inc.; BNI International (2,700 chapters internationally); and Ali Lassen's Leads Club (5,500 members, 400 chapters), to name just a few. These organizations have local chapters and also hold national meetings, conventions, and training sessions.

In addition, numerous local networking groups operate throughout the country. Some of these groups may be affiliated with national, state, or other local organizations, but many are simply single units that were created to facilitate the building of relationships on a wide range of interests. Besides those dedicated to business, other networking groups focus on interests that range from dating to promoting book sales. Network groups require an investment of time and money, but most members consider them to be wise investments in themselves.

Types of Networking Groups

We selected five network-focused groups to provide a sampling of the range of networking groups, their approaches, and how they operate. The groups profiled are:

- Network Associates, Inc.
- Caterina Rando's Circle of Eight
- The Hubbel Group
- AmSpirit Business Connections
- eWomenNetwork

Network Associates

Steve Krauser runs seven networking groups in New York and New Jersey under the banner of Network Associates. His father, Harvey Krauser, operates four Network Associates groups in Florida. Each Network Associates group has an average of twenty to twenty-five members, men and women, who pay an annual $2,000 fee. Each group meets once a month. They meet on a regularly scheduled day, such as the first Tuesday of the month, and at a set time like 8 A.M. to 10 A.M. Meetings are held at a conference hall and members sit around circular tables. Steve Krauser presides from the front of the room.

In a group, the career fields represented might include a stockbroker, computer consultant, real estate and personal injury attorney, mortgage banker, telephone system consultant, etc. Members join Network Associates as businesses, which enables more than one member of a business to attend meetings.

Guests

To ensure a good mix, Steve Krauser regularly asks members to identify businesses that are not represented in the group and whether representatives of those industries should be invited to meetings as guests. Early each year, Steve posts the schedule of meetings for the year. Prior to each meeting, he sends out memos reminding members about the meeting and informing them about the program so that they can prepare.

One-to-One Visits

It's essential that group members understand what other members do because if they don't, they can't make good referrals. To ensure such understanding, each member is required to make a one-to-one visit to another member's place of business. Visits usually consist of tours and question-and-answer sessions. During one-to-one visits, the visiting members must give hosts sufficient time to explain what they do, what differentiates them from others in their industry, and what their style or approach is with clients. Visiting members must receive sufficient information for them to identify opportunities for the host and to know where they can implant the host in their contact base. Some members accomplish this in one visit, while others need multiple visits.

One-to-one visits also help members identify problems that their existing clients may be having. Then they can draw from the expertise of the group to solve those problems, which is "networking at the highest level," according to Steve. Once a year, all seven of the Network Associates groups assemble at a larger venue. Krauser calls this the Network of Networks. Occasionally, he will hold other off-site events such as golf outings.

Rules and Referrals

Network Associates does not allow members to solicit each other's business and doing so is grounds for automatic expulsion. However, members can approach each other for help or to use each other's services. For example, a mortgage broker can't solicit another member's business, but the broker can hire the telephone consultant to design a phone system for his or her office. The group does not permit remuneration between members. So, if you close a deal after receiving a lead from a group member, you can't give them money or even a gift. The only return should be thanks and referrals.

The group also serves as a resource for its members. When a member, Larry Turell, a life and health insurance whiz, was thinking of refinancing his home, he asked the advice of a mortgage banker who was a member of the group. The banker volunteered to talk with Larry, at no charge, and taught Larry the questions to ask when seeking a mortgage. As a result of the group member's help, Larry was able to get a terrific deal and avoid a lot of the aggravation usually entailed in refinancing.

The Meetings

Network Associates has formal business meetings, which Steve leads. Steve starts the formal proceedings by going around the room and asking members to give a short sound bite stating who they are and describing their business. Frequently, he will ask members to add to their sound bite by telling the group about their most interesting business experience that month, their most recent business transaction, or problems they are encountering in their industry.

The next session is called "Getting Down to Business," which generally takes at least an hour. Steve asks the group, "Does anyone have anything that they're working on that you may need assistance with?" Everyone at the meeting, members and guests alike, then has the opportunity to explain what help he or she needs and what project of theirs has problems. The other members may offer direct help or suggestions, or refer the member to someone in their networks who might help. The Getting Down to Business segment is the time during the meeting when all of the members have the opportunity to use the entire group.

After the Getting Down to Business segment, a five-minute coffee break follows. During this time, members can follow up on matters raised in the Getting Down to Business portion of the meeting. Steve then conducts ten to fifteen minutes of networking exercises to help the group polish their networking skills.

The final meeting segment covers two areas: (1) reports on one-to-one visits and (2) exchanging thanks. Members tell the group about their one-to-one visits and what they learned so others can share their insights about the host's business. Network Associates teaches its members that whenever they make a one-on-one visit, the visitor should give the host a lead. It's a way of saying thanks and of giving, which is so essential in networking.

During the final segment, members have the opportunity to thank others for giving them leads in the past or at this meeting. It's also the time to identify other members whose businesses you want to visit. For example, if one member is being thanked often, it shows that the member is doing something right and that he or she is probably a great candidate for a one-on-one visit.

Caterina Rando's Circle of Eight

Business success coach and author Caterina Rando was looking for innovative ways to get better results—faster, and with less energy and resource output. An area that challenged her was how businesspeople could generate qualified leads: find potential clients for their products or services. As a result, she devised a solution that she believes produces more leads and enhances members' careers in less time and for just pennies a day. Rando says her idea is innovative because "It works for anyone, anywhere, on any budget."

The genesis of the Circle of Eight came from the book *The Tipping Point*, in which author Malcolm Gladwell detailed studies that showed that people easily remember seven things. For example, if ten different people who were standing in front of you suddenly vanished, you would easily recall seven of them. Additionally, Rando cites research that found that members of leads-exchange groups usually have seven people with whom they consistently exchange reciprocal leads.

Size Matters
The relatively small size of a Circle of Eight (seven others and you) is what makes it controllable and not unwieldy. Members can communicate easily, develop closer relationships, learn about each other's businesses and needs, and be alert for leads for other Circle members. A Circle of Eight is inexpensive to launch and maintain. You select seven complementary partners for your Circle and tap into their networks, smarts, experience, and resources.

To create a Circle of Eight, identify companies or individuals who provide a different, but complementary, product or service from what you provide. Also make sure that your Circle members are all seeking the same customer profile. Select members whom you trust, like, respect, and with whom you will be happy to be identified. Choose carefully because if one or two members don't measure up, the Circle could collapse or, worse yet, your reputation could be tarnished.

You should pick compatible partners, who are involved in businesses that will work with your group. For example, an interior designer who specializes in office design might invite into her Circle of Eight an architect, a painting contractor, an office-furniture dealer, an electrical contractor, a floor-covering firm, a landscape architect, and a lighting-fixtures company.

In a Circle of Eight, meetings are held via the phone on a conference or bridge line. Forty-five minute sessions are scheduled every two or three weeks to keep connected, ask questions, and exchange ideas. Members can network with other members from all over the country without leaving their offices and be the first to learn of regional trends that they could import. Rando assembled eight experts/speakers from different regions throughout the United States and Canada for her Circle. In your Circle of Eight, you can partner with firms that are based anywhere instead of being forced to partner with nearby firms of lesser value. You can seek out the best wherever they are located.

As soon as a Circle member comes across a lead, he or she circulates it electronically to all members. This allows Circle members to get leads quickly and act immediately on those that interest them. With seven other people beating the bushes for leads for you, your opportunities will multiply. Since all information is sent directly to your computer, you can easily categorize, calendar, and file it, which helps you stay well organized.

A Circle member is selected to be the facilitator for each meeting. When circle members get together by phone for their sessions, they follow a regular agenda. Sessions start with each member giving a quick report on the status of his or her business. Then each member informs the group how many leads, resources, or strategic referrals they have given the other members. In the Circle, a *lead* is something that turns into financial remuneration; a *resource* is someone or something that can provide help; and a *strategic referral* is something that will help a member, but does not involve payment—for example, speaking at an event that does not pay a fee, but will boost the member's career.

During the sessions, members report on how much they made from referrals from the Circle. They also tell the other Circle members how many leads they will provide and how many speeches they will book by the next Circle meeting. In addition, members discuss projects they have heard about in areas of interest to Circle members. They also find out about other Circle members' needs or interests and areas where they can partner, refer, or help. Members can brainstorm ideas, share referrals, and connect other members to both current and past clients who might be interested in a Circle member's services. Members also discuss innovations in their respective industries, which could work for other members.

Members can also provide each other with resources. They can recommend vendors, share cost-cutting and technical innovations, and inform other members about trade shows and other upcoming events of interest. Members can also enter into cooperative marketing ventures, such as partnering on mailings or ads that would be prohibitively expensive for any one member.

Circles of Eight usually become circles of friends because the members seek and depend upon each other for advice and resources. Each Circle member gains valuable support because the other members serve as his or her sounding boards, board of directors, expanded sales force, and allies. The key feature of a Circle of Eight is that all members actively search for opportunities that will advance the other members and their businesses.

The Hubbel Group

The Hubbel Group was a loosely knit, grass-roots women's group that sprang to life in Spokane, Washington, and which enjoyed a remarkably productive five-year run. In that time, it enriched many women's lives and profoundly changed the community.

In 1997, Julia Hubbel's world collapsed: She lost her job, lost her land, got divorced, and ended up living in Spokane, Washington, with few friends, contacts, or prospects. Plus, her health was a serious mess. Desperate for work, she joined every organization, networked like mad, and sent out 400 resumes. She got one interview, but not the job. She filed for bankruptcy and lost her house, car, credit rating, career, her dogs, and her self-respect—everything but her gumption.

While Hubbel's life was falling apart, the seeds of her networking started to sprout. In her travels, she met wonderful women who were at the top of their fields: entrepreneurs, community leaders, senior regional directors, executive vice presidents, artists, writers, dancers, and university professors. Through her networking efforts, Hubbel realized that these women needed to meet each other and form a support group and that she could make it happen.

Hubbel scheduled lunch with one of the women and was so impressed that she couldn't wait to introduce her to other women she had been getting to know. The next time they met for lunch, a third woman joined them and "it was over-whelming." By the fourth lunch, nine women showed up, all handpicked from Hubbel's growing list of friends/contacts. None knew each other, but they instantly liked, respected, and realized that they needed each other. So, they agreed to meet regularly.

Within three years, the group grew to sixty members, with a core group of about sixteen who were the most active. In between meetings, Hubbel networked to recruit potential members.

Originally they called themselves the Great Broads, but they changed the name to the Hubbel Group in order to appear more professional. Hubbel personally interviewed each new candidate over a cup of coffee to see if she would fit. During interviews, Hubbel tried to spot the woman's needs and connect her to group members who could help, even those women who did not join. Age was not a determinative factor and members ranged from twenty-seven to fifty-four. The requirements for membership were brains, accomplishments, skills, an understanding of the need to give for the larger good, and the need to learn how to receive from other women. The women who joined did so to serve and make a difference.

The group charged no dues; the only requirement was that the women show up and be totally present for the ninety-minute lunches held once a month. At meetings, the women went around the table and answered a set of questions, staying within a strict time frame in order to give everyone a turn.

At meetings, each woman:

- Told the group what she did better than anyone, without using "I think," or "I guess," or other wishy-washy lan-guage. The sentence had to begin with "I'm the best _____" so the others would know what she had to offer.

- Told the group about a recent event she wanted to celebrate: a contract, a promotion, a political appointment, a job offer, a new grandchild, or anything else that she wished to share with the group.
- Told the group about updates or news of interest to the members such as a high-level dinner, a political campaign needing volunteers, a job posting, or whatever might have an impact on the group members' lives.
- Asked for help from the group. According to Hubbel, this was by far the hardest part. The women asked for advice on potentially difficult legal situations at work, marketing an e-mail list, or referrals for a job; it didn't matter. The group members, who were powerful women, competed to brainstorm and put forth the best solutions.

On the first Friday of each month, the group hosted a regular potluck dinner. The potluck allowed them to spend hours at a member's house and further develop their relationships. As they grew closer, they laughed with each other, provoked each other, promoted each other, and grew with each other.

Over time, the Hubbel Group provided referrals to local boards and placed a woman on the Chamber of Commerce Board. They mentored young women coming out of the military to help them find high-paying corporate jobs. They supported each other through divorces, job shifts, and location changes.

In 2000, Julia Hubbel moved to Colorado to be close to her ailing mother. The group found another leader and continued to meet for another eighteen months. Since then, the friendships formed in the group have remained intact, but the group dissolved.

"The most important lesson I learned through the Hubbel Group," says Julia, "was that when I believed I had nothing to give, I discovered that I had everything to give. When I had hit rock-bottom and was facing living out of a cardboard box on the street in a city far from family and friends, I found a way to be of service. And through the Hubbel Group, I discovered that when everything else is stripped away, all the trappings of power and influence that we believe that are so powerful, all people really want from us is to be acknowledged and valued. By providing that to these powerful women, and by putting them together and helping to foment their relationships through celebration and storytelling, we changed much more than many women's lives. We helped change the face of a community."

AmSpirit Business Connections

AmSpirit Business Connections is an organization that helps sales representatives, entrepreneurs, and professionals succeed by creating a forum where they can exchange qualified referrals. The focus of AmSpirit is giving to others and enabling members to serve as resources for their customers and clients. In doing so, AmSpirit members have the opportunity to meet other professionals they would not otherwise meet, while improving their business communication skills.

"A qualified referral" is being given the name of a person or firm that will be expecting your call. The object is for members to put one another in touch with legitimate business opportunities that will further their careers.

As we go to press, AmSpirit has nearly fifty chapters, but it is engaged in a dynamic expansion program that is expected to add at least twenty chapters annually. It is seeking entrepreneurial-minded individuals to serve as organization directors.

The Logistics

Chapters vary in size and average about fifteen members per chapter and include both men and women. They meet weekly for regularly scheduled morning meetings—for example, from 7:30

to 8:45 A.M. on every Thursday. Chapters meet in a wide variety of public meeting spaces. Members have one-on-one luncheon meetings once a month as well as periodic social events. Chapters also have Web sites and publish monthly newsletters.

Only one member from a business category can belong to a chapter. Therefore, for example, a chapter can have only one landscaper, one jeweler, and one dentist. To join AmSpirit, applicants pay a $210 initiation fee and quarterly membership dues of $60. If the four quarterly membership payments are paid at one time, members get a discount and pay only $215.

The members of each chapter have the right to determine who will be accepted for membership.

Meetings

AmSpirit has structured meetings that all chapters basically follow. When members arrive at meetings, they are encouraged to greet everyone and shake hands. In one chapter, members can be fined 25 cents for not shaking hands. The members then have coffee, mingle, and network.

The president, who is chosen by chapter members, kicks off each meeting by asking another member to read the chapter's charter. The charter sets forth the purpose of the organization; reading it focuses the members and gives guests an overall understanding of the organization's objectives. The president then asks members who have brought guests to introduce them. The guests have the opportunity to stand up, tell the group what they do, and explain how the group can help them. Guests usually speak for two to three minutes. Chapter officers then report on developments in their area. For example, the officer in charge of scheduling the chapter's programs will announce the list of speakers for the next few meetings.

After the officers report, the chapter program begins. Each week, a chapter member will give a presentation about his or her business. In the presentation, the member will describe the benefits the business provides and tell the members what they need.

In most chapters, the presentations last for twenty minutes, but others schedule two speakers for ten minutes each. AmSpirit chapters do not use outside speakers. Occasionally, a chapter may decide not to have a speaker and the central AmSpirit organization will provide them with training materials on networking or the central organization's staff will conduct networking training.

After the chapter program, new members will be introduced, given membership certificates, and final announcements will be made. All of the members will then give a short introduction, talk briefly about their business and their needs, and make referrals. If they received referrals from people at the meeting, they will thank and update them about the referrals.

Operating Philosophies

According to AmSpirit's Regional Director, Frank Agin, "There is a formula behind networking. It's like being healthy. We know what it takes to be healthy: Drink eight glasses of water each day, exercise, and eat a balanced diet and chances are you'll be healthy. The formula for networking is that you give referrals; you get to know, like, and trust people in your network; let them get to know, like, and trust you; and give a concise, clear message as to who you are and what you do. This is what we teach. If you do these things, you raise the likelihood of your success tenfold."

AmSpirit members are asked to give at least two qualified referrals each month, which is seldom a problem. Those who don't give qualified referrals generally end up dropping out. Either of the two expected monthly, qualified referrals may be given to members of other AmSpirit chapters.

"The great networking stories are those of people who join the organization and slug away and persevere at building relationships," Agin explains. "Not the quick successes. A Realtor in one of our chapters has been in the organization for ten years. For the first two years, he didn't get a single referral, but he stuck with it, built relationships and did what needed to be done. Since that initial drought, he has sold upwards of 200 homes because of referrals he received directly through the organization."

Members are encouraged to do business with one another. If you don't have a travel agent, you are encouraged to use one who is in your chapter or another AmSpirit chapter. Soliciting other members is frowned upon and difficult to police. Members tend to join the organization because they don't like the typical sales approach, so aggressive solicitations are rare and usually backfire. Referral fees are not prohibited, but they are not encouraged. The organization is founded on the premise that members should give without expectation and the practice of giving referral fees creates expectations; an exception exists in the case of large corporations that have a referral fee program in place. Most members refer clients to other members because they trust the other member to serve their client well, which makes the referring member look good to his or her client.

eWomenNetwork

eWomenNetwork, Inc. (eWN), is an organization headquartered in Dallas, Texas, that connects female business owners and professionals with one another. It supports, promotes, and showcases its members' products and services and helps them achieve their professional objectives. eWomenNetwork teaches that networking is the art of giving and searching for ways to serve the needs of others before focusing on yourself. It instructs members to be "other-focused."

The organization bills itself as "the #1 resource for connecting and promoting women and their businesses worldwide." It also claims to be the "fastest growing membership-based professional women's networking organization in North America."

"We are the marketing machine for women-owned businesses and corporate professionals," eWN cofounder and CEO Sandra Yancy states. "Every initiative we take on must answer the question, 'Does it connect women and does it promote them?'"

Membership

eWN has seventy-five chapters across North America and is rapidly expanding. Members join the national organization, not merely the local chapters, so they can attend meetings or events at any eWomenNetwork venue. Both individual and corporate memberships are offered.

An applicant pays a one-time lifetime $290 initiation fee. She then pays $16.95 per month for membership benefits, which includes having her business profiled on the eWomen Network.com Web site and having a link created from eWomen-Network.com to her personal or business Web site. Under its Three For Free program, the initiation fee will be refunded if a member, at any time during the term of her membership, recommends three new members who are profiled on the Web site.

With their membership, women get two complementary coaching sessions from eWN's Premier Success Coaches, who are all certified and experienced coaches. Coaches specialize in a number of areas such as coaching for moms, coaching for creativity, and coaching from the legal perspective, which is provided by an attorney. Members also have access to eWN's premier faculty, which is composed of noted authors and experts in a number of diverse fields.

Business Platform

eWN has a multifaceted business platform. The parts of the organization include:

1. The Web site—eWomenNetwork.com has the world's largest photographic database of women entrepreneurs and women professionals. It gets 3 million hits per month. The site contains profiles of eWN's members and their contact information. Members can post three images with their profile and the eWN database is searchable by names, business categories, and geographical areas.

2. Chapter meetings—Accelerated Networking Events (ANEs, which are chapter meetings) take place at each of the seventy-five chapters across North America once each month. ANEs are either luncheon events or late afternoon/evening receptions and last for two hours. Meetings contain structured networking rounds. In round one, each woman is given a card with a number from one to eight; she is told to find all the other women who have the same number and sit with them in a circle. In the circles, each woman is given two minutes to state who she is, what service or product she provides, and what she wants in the next thirty days. Members are encouraged to identify who they know who could help other members. "Men do business based on reports, women do business based on rapport," Robin Ramsey, eWN's Managing Director for San Francisco, declares.

Quest for the Best

Sandra Yancy needed an engraver in the Dallas area. The eWomenNetwork International Conference was fast approaching and the organization would be presenting a lot of gifts that needed to be engraved. She checked the eWN membership, but couldn't locate a member who was a local engraver, so she went to the forum. Yancy posted a request for referrals to an engraver in the Dallas area and within forty-eight hours, she had eleven recommendations. From these recommendations, Yancy found her engraver, who did a wonderful job. "That's the beauty of online networking!" Yancy exclaimed.

After lunch and another round of structured networking, the final ANE segment is the raffle, which is designed to familiarize the group with the members' products or services. "We always hear women say, 'If people would try my products, I know they would like and buy them,'" Yancy reports. "So, we raffle their products and services to provide that chance."

3. Radio programming—The eWomenNetwork Radio show is broadcast live every Sunday from 8 to 9 P.M., central time. It is carried on the number-one ABC affiliate in the nation and can be heard in 80 percent of the country. Plus, the programs can be heard live on the Internet. The purpose of the radio show, which is hosted by Sandra Yancy, is to spotlight eWN members and to create greater awareness of them.

4. Print publications—eWN has affiliate alliances and cross-promotes with women's publications across the nation. These publications run ongoing ads for the eWomenNetwork and publish articles and information about the organization and its members. In turn, eWN promotes the publications to its members.

5. Nonprofit eWomenNetwork Foundation—This nonprofit foundation helps women in need and also conducts a "fementoring" program for young women in high school and college. The purpose of the foundation is to nurture up-and-coming women who will become the business leaders of tomorrow.

In addition to its other activities, eWN also runs several major events. Among them are its annual international conference, which usually lasts four days, a holiday extravaganza that is generally held the first Thursday of each December, and one-day Business Exchanges and Expos for the chapters.

Action Steps

1. List the five organized groups in your area where you could best network.

   _____

   _____

   _____

   _____

2. State your three major objectives in joining organized networking groups.

   _____

   _____

   _____

3. Set forth the features of organized networking groups that appeal to you.

   _____

   _____

   _____

   _____

4. List features of organized networking groups that you wish to avoid.

   _____

   _____

   _____

Eleven

Evaluating Networking Groups and Events

THIS CHAPTER WILL COVER:

The selection process

Return on investment

Seminal questions

Maintaining the connection

Reviewing productivity

"The success of each is dependent
upon the success of the other."
—John D. Rockefeller Jr.

The number of networking groups and networking events is overwhelming. Each is unique and promises to deliver special benefits that you can't possibly live without. Joining and attending all of them is impossible and even if you could join them all, it would bankrupt you. So you must be extremely selective.

Unfortunately, being selective isn't so easy. It's a complicated process that takes more than simply signing up with a group recommended by your most trusted buddies or the first group or event that appeals to you. A number of underlying factors complicate the evaluation process. They are as follows:

As a rule, the benefits of networking groups increase in direct proportion to the regularity of your attendance. Maximum benefits usually flow when you become a fixture at group meetings and events. When you attend regularly, you get in position to network with the best because you have become a part of the in-group, the inner circle. You become privy to the inner workings of the organization and its future plans. When you're in the inner circle, people will think of you when they think about the group or its events. As a regular attendee, you can meet and build closer relationships with key organization members and nonmembers who come in contact with the group. Usually, your prominence in the organization increases with time and the degree of your involvement, as does your visibility. If you only attend every other meeting, chances are that you will reap fewer and less meaningful benefits than if you attend every meeting. If you attend only occasionally, expect occasional benefits.

You should realize several basic facts when considering networking groups. First of all, networking groups are always in flux. Members come and go or attend irregularly, which changes the organization's dynamic. As a result, the leadership and the group's agenda also change. In addition, the objectives of groups can also shift with the success or failure of how the group's projects and events are received. While an influx of new members can breathe life into a static old group and get it moving in exciting new directions, it can also cast faithful established members off to the side and out of the loop. Features that initially drew you to the group may no longer exist and it may feel like you belong to a different group than the one you thought you joined. Like people, organizations also bog down, become stale, tired, and dated. Causes that were once vital and compelling are eclipsed by new and more pressing concerns, which may not interest or serve you. Overall, organizations can be of varying value to you at different times and it's hard to predict when those times will occur.

Secondly, you can spread yourself too thin. If you try to attend too many group meetings and events, you'll give few, if any, the time and attention they deserve. Most likely, you'll end up wasting your valuable time and money. In addition, it will be physically exhausting and the energy you need for other endeavors will be sapped. By spreading yourself so thin, you might give other group members the impression that you're not giving their pet group or event your full effort and attention.

Finally, those who recommend groups and events may have different agendas than you. They may be involved in a group to increase their business while you want to serve your community; they may want publicity while you want anonymity; they may want to socialize and get dates, while you may not be in the market. In addition, group members often work to enlist new blood to increase their own clout within the organization. They may fudge it when they describe what you're going to get and when you join, you may find yourself smack-dab in the middle of a political brawl. Groups that your best pals truly love may not be the best fit for you or the best use of your resources.

The Selection Process

Most people select networking groups and events by identifying a few contenders and trying each out. If they like a group and it seems productive, they stick with it. However, as we have said, groups constantly change and you frequently must participate for a time before the maximum benefits kick in.

A better approach is researching each prospective networking group or event in depth before you join or attend. Identify the reasons why each group or event is attractive to you. Then list your objectives and be specific.

• Whom do you want to meet? Name the precise people or categories of people. If you want to network with the best, it's essential to (1) identify the groups and events they attend and (2) the groups and events that will give you the greatest opportunity to meet and build relationships with them.
• Do you want to meet others in your field, businesspeople from other industries, or do you want to join groups that provide services and help in the community?
• What do you expect to get from each event? Be specific. List your actual goals in detail: to double my business, to spend time in intelligent discussions about films, or to make new friends.

Consider whether the groups and events that interest you will be convenient or whether they will disrupt other important parts of your life. Are they held at places you can easily reach and at times that you can make? Will you have to rearrange your

Fun Matters

In making your selections, don't discount the enjoyment factor. People who have fun network more effectively. Spending time enjoyably adds to the quality of your life; it makes you anticipate, feel enthusiastic about, and look forward to upcoming meetings and events. People who are happy tend to be more relaxed, approachable, and attractive to others. Most folks prefer to be around happy people as opposed to grumps. If you enjoy the groups and events you attend, you will be more enthusiastic, which will enable you to communicate your desires with more passion.

life in order to attend and if so, is it worth it to you? Are there more convenient alternatives? Convenience is important. Don't obligate yourself to attend a meeting or event that could end up being more trouble than it's worth because, in time, you'll probably stop attending.

Usually, the first consideration in the selection process is identifying whom you can meet. Select your targets and remember to try to connect with the best. If you want to meet the top people in your industry, think about trade and industry associations. For example, if you're a lawyer, it makes sense to join the American Bar Association; if you're a female entrepreneur, consider the National Association of Women Business Owners; and if you're a graphic designer, try the American Institute of Graphic Arts.

At meetings and events sponsored by trade and industry associations, you can meet your peers, discuss common problems such as recent changes in the industry, and even develop working or referral arrangements. You can serve on committees that can increase your visibility within your business, industry, and community. With greater visibility, you can meet and work with the policy- and decision-makers and extend your network to the higher echelons of your field. By becoming an asset to the organization, you can meet, work with, and form tight relationships with the leaders in your field.

If you want to meet people who are in different businesses, try business-oriented groups such as your local Chamber of Commerce, eWomenNetwork, IBI Global, or AmSpirit Business Connections. These organizations provide outstanding opportunities to cross-market your goods or services because they cater to people from a wide mix of businesses. If you have a product or service that would fit well with another industry, think about joining organizations or attending events directed at compatible industries. For example, an ambitious flower arranger should consider attending association meetings for wedding planners, funeral directors, and event organizers. If you want to establish a strong community base, think about joining service groups, as well as community, civic, or religious groups.

After you've identified the networking groups or events that might work for you, ask the members of your network for their opinions before signing up. Learn if they have attended the group's meetings or events and if not, do they know others who have. Also ask them if they can identify the best people for you to meet.

When you connect with others who have attended groups and events, ask them for a descriptive overview. Pay close attention to what they describe first and the level of their enthusiasm. Then zero in on the details: how many people attended, where the group met, how it was organized, how long meetings ran, did they follow a formal agenda, what items were on the agenda, and what was the tone of the meeting? Was it lighthearted, all business, formal, casual, or competitive? Did many people participate or did a few hog the floor? Was there a mixer or social component and if so, when did it take place and were the members or attendees accessible, warm, and friendly? As we previously stressed, the objectives of those you question may be different from yours. So factor that in before making your decision.

Return on Investment

In selecting which groups to join or events to attend, analyze whether it is a smart investment of your time and resources. Hellen Davis, President of Indaba Training Specialists, Inc., and author of *The 21 Laws of Influence*, is one of the most successful networkers we know. She graciously contributed the following gems when we interviewed her for this book.

Davis says, "I only attend organized networking events if I can anticipate a 500-percent return on my investment (ROI)—my investment being the cost of the event and, most importantly, my time. I learned early on that networking events can be expensive, especially when you're first starting in business or are on a limited budget. And I learned that the cost of the event has to be factored in as ROI. If you're weighing whether to go to one event that costs $50 or another that is $250, determine which should return a better ROI. Just because an event is inexpensive doesn't mean that you will get a better ROI. It might be more advisable to spend the extra money and attend the more expensive event rather than two or three less costly networking affairs."

Hard Costs

Hard costs are your purchases for participating in networking groups. What type of hard costs should you factor in? In calculating hard costs, include the price of admission, parking fees, and transportation expenses such as gas, vehicle, and maintenance expenses. In addition, to get the most out of events, you must be well prepared. So purchase all business materials that are appropriate to properly prepare you for the event. Calculate all of the above expenditures as hard costs.

Soft Costs

Soft costs are the opportunity costs and the cost of your time. Focus on the soft costs by asking the following questions:

- Is attending this event the best use of my time?
- Who do I hope to meet?
- Will this event draw the best people?
- Do I have a realistic expectation of doing business over either the short or long term?

If you earn $500 per day and will have to spend four hours at the event, your return from attending the event should be—at the very least—$1,250, plus the recovery of your hard costs.

Calculation: At $500 per day, four hours of your time is worth $250. $250 x 500% yields a ROI factor of $1,250.

If you plan to stay in business, be realistic and select the events you decide to attend by calculating the anticipated ROI. Ask yourself, "Is this the best use of my time? Can I get a better ROI if I spend my time networking elsewhere?"

Essential Questions

Before you sign up for a networking event, there are several questions you must answer. They are:

- Who do I expect to meet at the event?
- Will someone on my Top 100 Prospecting List be in attendance?
- If so, will I have the opportunity to meet him or her?

The opportunity to meet someone high on your Prospecting List can be reason enough to attend an event. If you've got the right names on your targeted Prospecting List, contacting one of them can yield more than a 500-percent ROI. To calculate the soft costs, ask the following questions:

- What would it cost in time and effort to try to meet that individual?
- How realistic would my chances of meeting him or her be?
- Would we have to be on the same charitable board to meet or have interaction?
- Are there less expensive and more beneficial ways to meet this person?
- If so, what are they?

A client of Davis's told her she was going to a book signing to meet and hopefully do business with a certain celebrity. Davis asked her client, "Can you meet the celebrity any other way?" She pointed out that the celebrity might not appreciate being pitched at a book signing and that it could do her client more harm than good to approach the celeb at an inappropriate place. Then she asked, "How much time would it take to get in the door another way? Who do you know who knows the celebrity or their gate-keepers—agent, TV station, director, author, etc.? Would you ever get the opportunity to meet them if you did not attend this event?"

As it worked out, the local ABC affiliate was the first station where the celebrity worked. Davis's client knew the news director who knew the station manager. Two months later the celebrity and Davis's client met for lunch in New York City, which was certainly better than a pitch at a book signing! Since that lunch they've built and maintained a strong relationship.

Maintaining the Connection

Hellen Davis understands that networking is about keeping in touch with people you meet and find interesting. So she maintains an extensive system in which she records their contact information and keeps current on their likes and dislikes—on both a business and personal level. Keeping up on her contacts helped Davis reap rewards from an event sponsored to attract more women to the Republican Party. Senator Robert Dole, who was running for the presidency, was the featured speaker.

Just before the program began, Davis found herself standing with a group of women at the rear of the hall because men occupied all the front rows. When Hellen joked about the irony of this arrangement, the women standing with her laughed uproariously. An event organizer rushed over to restore decorum and Davis let him in on the joke. The organizer turned crimson, rushed up front, evicted the men, and replaced them with Davis and the female standees. When Senator Dole appeared, he immediately commented on how wonderful it was to see so many women in attendance.

After the program, the CEO of a large utility company complimented Davis on her initiative. The event organizer thanked Davis for saving his job and the utility company chief suggested that he get Davis on the news. Davis and the executive then agreed to meet for lunch the following week. The event organizer introduced Davis to a producer for *Dateline* who was there with a film crew from the local network affiliate to cover the event. They interviewed Davis for *Dateline* and the local news.

That evening, Davis's interview ran locally, but her *Dateline* spot was cut. The next day two clients called who had seen her interview. One set up a meeting for the following week through which Indaba landed a substantial contract. The other client confirmed that Indaba was on the short-list to provide sales training for their medical representatives in three countries. Two days later, he called again and told Davis that the contract was hers.

At lunch the following week with the utility company CEO, Davis learned that he was on the board of a large insurance company. Through his referrals, Indaba received contracts to train the company's home office employees. Indaba still provides that service. Subsequently, three of the company's executives went to work for other corporations and all hired Indaba to provide consulting, executive coaching, and training.

Every once in a while, Davis would pop an e-mail off to the *Dateline* producer and eventually they became friends and traded jokes. On several occasions, Davis hooked the producer up with experts and speakers even though she knew that she would not directly benefit. She helped the producer in order to keep the communication channels open.

Two years after the Republican event, a newsworthy story came to light that Davis thought *Dateline* might be interested in airing. So she called the producer. Because of the relationship they had established, the producer immediately returned her call. The next week, Davis was interviewed on *Dateline* and this interview ran. Immediately after it ran, CNN, *Extra*, *Philly After Midnight*, and many other radio and TV stations called and interviewed her. Davis calculates that she received over $400,000 worth of free airtime through her *Dateline* and local appearances and attributes it all to her maintaining contact with the producer.

Davis has also calculated what the original meeting at the Republican event produced. To date, in less than ten years, Indaba has received over $3 million in contracts and media exposure as a result of Davis's ability to network from that meeting. Davis continues to meet with the utility company's CEO on a regular basis. Whenever they meet, she brings him up to date on the latest branch of the referral tree that they first planted back in 1996. The CEO loves to hear about the people Davis has met through that one event and through his contacts. And guess what? He keeps referring her to his business associates!

Reviewing Productivity

Since groups change, as do your needs, review the productivity of the groups and events you attend. After you've been in a group for three months, review whether your membership has been fruitful. If it was, calculate the precise financial return to date and prospective future revenues.

As we mentioned previously, Jill sets firm targets for every networking event that she attends. Prior to attending a networking meeting, she sets the number of new people she wants to meet and the dollar amount of the business she hopes to transact. She actually sets two figures, her "go for" amount (a high target) and her promised amount (the realistic figure she must achieve). Every month, Jill reviews the networking events she attended to see if she met her benchmark projections. If she did not, she seriously considers whether or not to continue attending the organization's events.

Jill understands that she often must make repeated appearances at certain networking events before they pay off and she factors that into her decisions. She also considers the other benefits that she receives, which could include supporting worthy organizations and/or causes, learning new information, or simply enjoying herself and having a good time.

Each month, when Jill measures her productivity, she "resets her counter to zero." In other words, she does not compare her results with those for the previous month. Such comparisons, she believes, cause unnecessary stress and don't produce an accurate measurement because they don't quantify the success that is attributable to her attendance at specific events.

If you decide to remain in the organization, review whether it is still worth your time and resources on a regular basis—at least every three months. Habits form easily. Warm friendships that you make with certain members can keep you involved in groups that no longer provide more essential benefits. If you're in it for the friendships, keep attending, but if your other objectives are not being met, it probably is time to move on.

Was It Worth It?

Examine whether the Medical Association annual dinner, the Elks Club picnic, or your service club's outing were worth your time and money. Again, don't minimize the enjoyment factor, especially with events. If you find that you truly enjoy certain groups or events, don't be too quick to deprive yourself of that pleasure. Having outlets that you enjoy can yield benefits that may be hard to envision now. So, treat yourself, give yourself the right to have fun, and let the network magic work.

Ask yourself:

- Are my group memberships still productive?
- Am I getting enough of a return to justify my membership?
- Is it a good investment of time, money, and energy?

If you are not seeing sufficient returns, it may be time to reassess or rotate your membership. By rotating you can continue as an organization member, but concentrate your focus elsewhere.

Action Steps

1. Identify the categories of people that you would like to meet at groups or events.

   _____

   _____

   _____

   _____

2. Are your group memberships still productive? If so, list why they are productive. If not, list why they are not productive.

_____

_____

_____

_____

3. List three groups or events and the return on investment of each.

_____

_____

_____

4. List five additional groups or events to investigate joining or attending.

_____

_____

_____

_____

_____

Twelve

The Internet and Special Tactics

THIS CHAPTER WILL COVER:

Web sites

Internet communities

Mailing lists

E-zines and newsletters

Recommended meeting lists

Remembering names

IBI Global's SNAP

"National borders aren't even speed bumps on the information superhighway."

—Tim May, ontologist

According to estimates, over 300 million people use or have access to the Internet. As a result, the Internet has become a networker's paradise because it enables networkers to link up with a virtually unlimited array of potential partners across the globe.

In the past, when you wanted to network, you were restricted to regional or industry-specific efforts. Usually, you had to network in your own community and try to build from there. A certain few were able to attend state or national trade shows, conferences, or conventions and could network within their own industry. However, most of these events were costly, and they took place only a few times each year. Building close relationships with contacts in other states or countries was difficult and expensive, so most networkers stayed close to home.

Now, this has all changed because the Internet recognizes few boundaries. In fact, the Internet erases most boundaries. Web sites and Internet communities now blanket the world. When you visit a site, it may be based abroad or down the street, and an Internet community may include local, national, and international members. As a result, your reach is expanded and you may have direct access to experts who have vast experience in a field you may have just entered.

The fact that the Internet reaches so many people dramatically increases the pool of potential network partners that you can access. By simply joining an Internet community, you can be surrounded by scores of like-minded people who could become members of your network.

As a networking tool, the Internet is an exceptional value. You don't have to pay steep admission fees or the expenses of attending networking groups and events. When you network via the Internet, you can sit at home, wearing whatever is comfortable, and network with multiple, faceless partners in cyberspace.

Web Sites

As we suggested in Chapter 7, Your Networking Toolkit, it is a great advantage to build a dynamic, information-based Web site. Fill it with the precise information that you would like the world to know about you, your product, or your service. Use your Web site to paint a striking picture that will intrigue potential network partners and attract them to you.

In constructing your Web site, be careful—a bad site is often worse than having no Web site at all. So make your Web site a good one. Make it better than good—make it great, because a great Web site will make you look great and keep visitors coming back. A site that lacks quality content, that is poorly designed, or is difficult to navigate will alienate visitors. Not only won't they revisit your site, they will complain about it to others.

If you want to attract the best people, design a fabulous Web site that the top people will recognize as great. If you are a tax lawyer, include items about taxation that will truly be of interest to you and to many others and that you would like to discuss and explore. If you are a musician, describe your influences and include features that could open up a dialogue with those who have similar interests. Craft your Web site and its design to attract and connect you with the type of visitors you seek, people who can share your interests and who can help you grow and succeed.

In designing your Web site, decide:

- Who constitutes your target audience?
- What value does your product and/or service provide them?
- What are your goals and objectives for your Web site?
- What is the best way to reach your target audience?
- What information will they need?

Don't put your Web site up until it's well tested and you are absolutely sure that your site is informative, attractive, and reflective of your mission. If using your site isn't totally painless for visitors to use, they will flee in droves and probably never come back.

The main reason why your Web site exists is to support your mission. Every element in it should support and reflect the mission of your business or whatever you're trying to promote. If the mission of your business is to sell candy, create a mouth-watering site that makes visitors want to bite into images on the screen. Clearly describe your candy and make it a snap for visitors to buy online.

Web Site Ideas

Among the many useful things that you can include on your site are: your portfolio, staff biographies, staff photographs, customer/client lists, news, newsletters, games, contests, privacy and security policies, and links to other sites. You should also include product descriptions, product specifications, price lists, photographs, illustrations, audio, video, ordering information, shipping instructions, a section for the media, and direct e-mail links for questions and comments or for ordering goods or services.

Internet Communities

According to estimates, hundred of thousands of Internet communities now exist—discussion groups, newsgroups, mailing lists, bulletin boards, message boards, chat rooms, and so on. Internet communities are interactive forums where members with similar interests exchange ideas and information. Although the term "discussion group" usually denotes a two-way conversation and the other terms refer to one-way dialogs, in this book, we'll simply use the term "discussion groups" to refer to all Internet communities and groups.

Discussion groups are ideal for networking because they basically are networks. They are electronic groups that share information and opinions on areas of mutual interest. Discussion group members can come from all over the world to conduct electronic conversations, build relationships, and help one another. In discussion groups, members network by:

- Exploring solutions to mutual problems
- Demonstrating their expertise
- Building relationships
- Building reputations
- Learning new things
- Helping one another

Internet discussion groups can expand your existing networks and link you with network partners throughout the world. Group members can post and respond to comments or simply sit back and silently observe. When you join a discussion group, you generally know little about the other members: who they are, what they do, and why they're in the group. But as you get more deeply involved, group members become friends, confidants, mentors, advisors, and valuable network partners. Before joining a Web community, answer the same questions that you asked when designing your Web site:

1. Who constitutes your target audience?
2. What is the best way to reach them?
3. What information will they need?
4. What value can I provide to the group to be recognized as an expert?

Decide who you want to connect with and who could help you the most. What industries are they in? Are there certain discussion groups within those industries that you could join? Identify the areas of your network that are weak and then identify groups in those areas that you could join to get you up to speed. To find discussion groups, see:

- *www.groups.google.com*   - *www.topica.com*
- *www.groups.yahoo.com*   - *www.dejanews.com*

Internet discussion groups can provide you with substantial information that can be invaluable to you and your network partners. From time to time you can monitor discussion groups, to learn what customers and clients are saying about you or your network partners' product or service and similar products and services. Monitoring discussion groups will also give you a feel for:

- Marketplace trends and conditions
- Needs and concerns of your network partners
- Problems with products and services
- How problems can be corrected
- Ideas for new products and applications
- Misinformation that you can dispel

Submit your own questions to discussion groups to get valuable feedback and to find kindred spirits. Through the feedback you receive you can identify potential network partners.

Mailing Lists

Mailing lists are hybrids that are a combination of electronic publications and Internet communities. They're easy to use and ideal for beginners. Basically, mailing lists are interactive discussion groups in which members send e-mails on subjects of mutual interest that are circulated to the other list members. Some lists moderate or screen messages while others distribute messages unscreened. Still other lists allow posting only by the owner of the list. You can build your network by contributing to mailing lists or starting your own. If you start your own mailing list, it can be purely commercial. You can freely send press releases and distribute information or promotional materials. Mailing lists can operate as separate networks or to solidify your contacts with business associates: employees, customers/clients, suppliers, retailers, and the media. Plus, they can enable list members to communicate directly with one another.

When you start a mailing list, you set the rules and chart the direction of the list. The interactive nature of mailing lists causes them to operate more like discussion groups. As with discussion groups, the tone, direction, and nature of mailing lists can shift with the addition and deletion of members, internal and external developments, and time.

Sites containing a list of mailing lists include:

- Do List—*www.dolist.net*
- Discussion Lists—*www.discussionlists.com*
- Point Arrow—*www.pointarrow.com*
- Publicly Accessible Mailing Lists—*www.paml.net*
- Tile.Net—*www.tile.net*
- Topica—*www.liszt.com*
- Web Scout Lists—*www.webscoutlists.com*

FAQs and Fact Sheets

Two elements that can be useful in many forms of Internet networking are FAQs and fact sheets. Create an FAQ, which is a list of frequently asked questions about yourself, your product, or your service, and their answers. Also write instructions for performing specific tasks or general fact sheets on your area of expertise, products, or services. Be informative. Establish your expertise and attract potential network partners by displaying your knowledge. You should:

- Include FAQs on your Web site
- Submit FAQs to discussion groups that permit them
- Turn FAQs into articles
- Update FAQs to reflect changes with you, your product, or service

Many discussion groups that do not allow advertising or self-promotion permit FAQs and useful information. FAQs can build your name recognition and establish you as an authority. Again, distribute FAQs only to discussion groups that accept them.

When you receive questions that your FAQs could not answer, obtain the questioner's contact information and answer them. If you think the question and answer would make a good addition to the FAQ list, add it. Hard questions also serve the purpose of informing you about problems with your products or materials, so formulate a policy for addressing the problems that will inevitably arise.

Add a form to your FAQ page so readers can e-mail questions to you that the FAQ may not have addressed. When you receive questions submitted on your form, you will know that they came from your FAQ page, which makes it easier to manage the information. You can also get the questioners' names and contact information in the event that you want to consider them for your network.

E-zines and Newsletters

A great way to keep in contact with your network is by creating electronic magazines (e-zines) or newsletters that you send via e-mail on a regular basis. Your e-zine can include information on developments in your industry, articles, book recommendations, guest columns, or a calendar of upcoming events. It can also include information about your business such as new services you now offer, your current client list, and profiles of your associates, prospects, and suppliers. Make your Web site e-zine/newsletter friendly. Design it so that visitors to your site can easily subscribe to your e-zine or newsletter—and make it just as easy for them to unsubscribe.

E-zines can be dynamic networking vehicles. If you have associates who have their own e-zines, you can trade favors. They can mention or include material promoting you or your product/service in their e-zine or newsletter, and, in turn, you can mention or include information about them in yours. By trading favors, you can support your network partners, cross-pollinate your e-zine/newsletter, generate additional subscribers, and get your information to a new group of potential customers/clients.

In addition, messages can be placed in e-zines for a fee, which is essentially paid advertising. However, in building and maintaining your network, it may be advisable to not charge to run other people's items. Chalk it up to building solid network relationships, which can remain fruitful long after the money you would have received has run out.

Special Tactics

In the course of writing this book, we came across a number of fascinating tactics that were primarily designed to facilitate and/or speed up the networking process. Most of these methods focused on achieving quick end results, not gradually developing close network relationships. Some tactics were inventive adaptations of standard networking practices that their advocates swear by and claim will produce outstanding results in short time spans.

In this chapter, we are including several of the special tactics that we consider most intriguing and adaptable. We know that all of these approaches won't work for everyone or in every situation. However, we hope that they will inspire you to create personally tailored versions that will help obtain the results you need.

As you read the following special tactics, use your imagination, be creative, and have fun. Picture how these tactics or parts of them could best serve you. You may even consider mixing and matching elements from each of the following approaches until you find a hybrid that works for you.

Recommended Meeting Lists

Author Leonard Koren was invited to an event celebrating the publication of a new book. When he arrived, he was handed a nametag and a card. His name was written on the card along with the statement, "People you should meet." Below that statement were the names of six individuals who the hosts thought would interest Koren. In the course of the evening, Koren met several of those on his list and did indeed find most of them interesting.

Although Koren met equally interesting people who were not on his list, the fact that each person was given a list took on a life of its own and became a topic of conversation. People talked about it all evening. Upon seeing others, they would check out his or her nametag and say, "Well, you're not on my list, but . . ." or "Oh, you're on my list," and enter into conversations.

If you're hosting a networking event, recommended meeting lists can be both helpful and fun. Basically, it's a larger version of planning the seating arrangement for a dinner. In both cases, your goal is to connect people on the basis of how you think they will relate, which is fun—especially when they hit it off. In addition, the novelty of recommending meeting lists can serve as a great conversation starter.

Preparing recommended meeting lists can be long, arduous work and requires great networking skills. Like any mix-and-match process, many connections will immediately seem obvious while some mavericks will seem hopeless and test your matchmaking skills. However, these strays often connect with kindred spirits and the most unlikely combinations can form the strongest relationships.

Recommended meeting lists force you to examine your guest roster, obtain knowledge about each guest, and find common denominators that can lead to good connections. If you're hosting large events it means lots of work. However, most guests will appreciate the time and effort you expended even if they hate the matches you recommended.

Remembering Names

During our research for this book, people repeatedly explained that they were not good networkers because they couldn't remember the names of people they met. Even successful networkers revealed that they constantly struggle to remember names. Most of them had some sort of a memory system that didn't work consistently, so we decided to turn to an expert.

Public speaker and marketing consultant Ken Glickman suffered from a faulty memory for names, so he created a system that has trained him to remember well over 100 first names. Glickman concentrates on first names, which he feels is sufficient for networking meetings and events. However, he makes it clear that his system is a short-term approach. Don't expect it to work when you come across someone out-of-context whom you met briefly last year at a conference.

According to Glickman, "Most people don't remember names because they don't really listen in the first place. However, they do remember people they like and admire because they pay attention to them. Everyone's favorite word is their own name. So if you want to make others feel important and good about themselves, call them by name." Glickman explains, "You can't make them feel special if you don't remember their name. And if you pretend to know someone's name, you're usually going to get caught and will no longer be seen as credible. People infer that if you're lying about that, you are untruthful about other things."

To address his inability to remember names, Glickman developed a three-step technique that forced him to concentrate and listen. By mastering Glickman's system, you can teach yourself to remember those you meet. You can also avoid embarrassing moments when you can't recall the name of someone you just met. Improving your memory for names should help you network with more success and confidence.

When Glickman meets someone new, he:

1. Deliberately shakes his or her hand and repeats his or her first name several times during their initial conversation. For example, he might say, "Joe, it's nice to meet you. Where are you from, Joe? And how long will you be here, Joe?" Or, he will introduce Joe to someone else and say, "Joe, this is Harry. Harry, Joe is here for the meeting."

2. As soon as he or she walks away, within ten to fifteen seconds, Glickman visualizes the person's face in his mind and repeats his or her name.

3. About thirty seconds later, Glickman looks around the room for that person, and, when he spots him or her, he says the person's name once more.

Glickman's process requires you to listen, focus, and connect the names and faces in your mind. The more you do it, the better you get.

When Glickman forgets people's names, he goes right up to them and states, "I've been having trouble remembering names," and he asks them their names. Glickman believes that when you admit not knowing their names, you can create a mental block and the quickest way to clear that block is to immediately ask.

Similarly, when you meet someone and can't remember his or her name, don't bluff or pretend. Promptly say, "I remember your face and I enjoyed our conversation so much last time, but I'm sorry I'm having trouble with names and I can't remember your name." Provide whatever context you can to show that you only forgot their name, not them. Then when they tell you their name, repeat it during the remainder of your conversation.

IBI Global's SNAP

IBI Global, Inc. has developed a trademarked accelerated networking process that it calls SNAP. Here's how it works.

At a networking meeting with fifty or more people, instead of networking by swapping business cards, five or six chairs are placed in a circle. There are no tables, only chairs. On the floor, in the center of each circle, are three items: (1) a large, brightly colored hat, (2) a glossy wand with a ball at one end, and (3) a stack of "See Me" cards, which we will describe below.

The participants in each circle are seated in the chairs facing each other with their knees a few inches from the neighbor next to them. The circles where participants initially sit are their home circles. One member of each circle is designated to go first and he or she puts on the hat.

The SNAP session begins when the designated member tells the other circle members, "Here's what I'm doing" and "Here's what I need next." Their messages should take no longer than ten to fifteen seconds and other members of the circle may ask questions that the speaker might use to sharpen his or her pitch. Speakers may use props such as photographs or illustrations of their work, copies of books or articles they have written, and samples of their products. They can also distribute cards or literature.

The key in delivering the message is to get right to the heart of the matter, clearly explain precisely what you need, and to not give extraneous information. When addressing circle members, participants should smile and connect with everyone in the circle, but move fast.

When the first speaker finishes delivering his or her message, the person seated to his or her left informs the other circle members what he or she is doing and what he or she needs. In turn, each circle member addresses the group until they go around the circle. The full round for all circle members to deliver their pitches takes only three minutes. The initial phase can be repeated twice to help all of the participants refine their messages.

After each circle member has delivered his or her pitch, the other members of the circle hand him or her a "See Me" card. The words "See Me" are printed across the top of the card followed by spaces where each participant writes his or her name, room number (if participants are staying at a conference), and e-mail address. Seasoned IBI participants and those in IBI's weeklong sessions often have preprinted stickers with their contact information and their picture. Below the contact information, the words "Yes! See Me! I am Your:" are printed in bold, uppercase letters. Below that line are three entries, which state:

- Solution for
- Introduction to a contact that will resolve your project (because I CAN influence them)
- Introduction to a contact that "Can" resolve your project (they CAN do it!—I'll introduce you today)

The first item tells the recipient, "I am the solution for your problem. I personally can provide what you need." The second item shows that the giving party has a contact who can provide the solution the recipient needs and that the giving party has influence over his or her contact's decisions. And the third item states that the giving party has a contact who can solve the recipient's problem, but the giving party does not influence his or her contact's decisions. It also conveys that the giving party will introduce the recipient to his or her contact today.

In the spaces provided after these three items, the giving party can write additional information. Or they can merely circle the letter on the card that indicates the level of help they can provide.

After giving See Me cards, the giving parties should make notes to themselves stating to whom they gave a card and the degree of help they indicated that they would provide and why. Therefore, when the recipient contacts them, they can remember why and how they thought they could help. IBI encourages participants to give freely and promotes giving back. So those who provide high-quality contacts can receive substantial returns including fees, stock, or both.

After the members go completely around their circle, the designated member, who is wearing the hat, stands up and runs around to the other circles. He or she jumps into seats vacated by other hat wearers, who have now moved to other circles. Hat wearers deliver their messages quickly and the circle members then give the hat wearer See Me cards listing the type of help they can provide. After receiving cards, or receiving no cards, the hat wearers move on to circles that they have not visited. The object is for the hat wearer to sit in as many different circles as possible. As the hat wearers run from circle to circle, some circles have a vacant seat. So members of those circles will wave the wands and call to hat wearers to inform them of the vacancy.

After a set time, usually three to five minutes, the hat wearer returns to his or her home circle and the hat is passed to the person seated to his or her left. When a signal is given, the new hat wearer starts racing around to give his or her pitch to other circles. The process continues until each member of the circle has worn the hat and delivered his or her message to other circles. This is super networking: the practice of going beyond your own network.

"Super networking is the master skill of the new century. It is the process by which you invite and capture the contacts of your expanding network," IBI cofounder Bernhard Dohrmann explains. "Your network is not used for who they are, but for who they know. In this process, you rapidly develop connections and contacts for your purpose or agenda of the moment, which is to solve priorities one at a time, not five at a time. You use your network to resolve the priority of the moment primarily by who they know, which means you're super networking. If you solve them by who they are, you're only networking. Those who know a little bit about networking skills will always be outperformed by those who know how to super network."

IBI teaches that who you know in your own circle doesn't matter, even though you may have some great cards and great contacts. What does matter is connecting with as many circles as you can and tapping into their resources.

After participants receive See Me cards, they must follow up. At SNAP sessions, people move so fast that they often need reminders to inform them why they offered help. The best approach is to contact them immediately after the SNAP session, show them their See Me card, and set a firm time for further contact.

At SNAP sessions, IBI prefers as wide a mix as possible because diverse backgrounds produce more contacts. Similarly, "SNAP works better with larger groups because you have more resources for connectivity," according to Dohrmann. "While most people ask for something that they want in the future, SNAP enables them to get what they need now," explains author Barry Spilchuk, an experienced SNAP session leader.

When IBI holds sessions for corporate clients, it asks them to bring their key subcontractors, suppliers, and vendors because they have insightful, creative solutions that companies can utilize. IBI believes that the presence of these resources help corporations remove roadblocks and develop customers. It also requests companies to bring their customers to SNAP sessions because customers will tell them how to get and satisfy more customers, if they'll only listen and let them.

Dohrmann believes that, "In a super networking session, you can accomplish more in 90 minutes than you ordinarily can in 90 days." He recommends that organizations hold SNAP sessions twice a year and require every participant to bring one new member or guest. If they do, Dohrmann is convinced that they will double the club's membership.

Action Steps

1. Identify the three target audiences that you would like your Web site or discussion group to attract.

_____

_____

_____

_____

2. List the information that your target audiences would need.

_____

_____

_____

_____

3. Set forth the best ways to reach your target audiences.

_____

_____

_____

_____

4. State what you, as a discussion group member, would want the group to provide for you.

_____

_____

_____

_____

Thirteen

Networking for Your Life

THIS CHAPTER WILL COVER:

Health care

Legal services

Financial services

Real estate

Job hunting

Dating

"(1) Out of clutter find simplicity,
(2) From discord find harmony,
(3) In the middle of difficulty
lies opportunity."

—Albert Einstein's
Three Rules of Work

The road you travel to find the best can be long and winding—even when you've got a great network. Often, the route is filled with bumps, wrong turns, detours, and plenty of dead ends. To help you on your journey, we've come up with specific suggestions in a number of categories to help you to find the best. Naturally, these suggestions are not the only ways to find the best, but they are approaches that can help you create a plan of attack that meets your particular needs. We hope these ideas stimulate your creativity and provide you with more ways of finding the best.

As we've previously stressed, what constitutes the best is always a subjective determination and depends on the particular people, time, and circumstances involved. What's the best for others might be dead wrong for you and what was the ultimate just last week might be unacceptable tomorrow. So gather lots of information, follow every lead, and check out every recommendation. Then examine all of your options and it should help you decide what the best is for you.

Health Care

Nothing is more important than your health and the health of those you love. When you look for a doctor, dentist, nursing home, home health agency, or other health-care provider, it's especially important to find practitioners, facilities, and approaches that give you and the patient (if it's not you) confidence. When it comes to health, someone's life may be on the line, so it makes good sense to try to obtain the very best. In addition, when patients have positive attitudes and believe in the course of treatment prescribed, their recovery rates increase.

Collect Names

First, speak with your primary care physician, and be sure to bring writing materials with you. Physicians who are established in the community know the top specialists and will give you names to call. Even if they don't provide names, they still know where to get that information and you should push them to do so. Because health care is so specialized, have your physician tell you the precise type of specialist you need in order for you to clearly explain your needs to others.

Ask your primary care doctor for three referrals. Have him or her rank their competence and briefly tell you something about each. Specifically, ask your doctor which one he or she would use in your situation, but don't be surprised if your doctor hedges or declines to give a specific answer.

Write down all of your doctor's answers; don't trust your memory. During health scares, concentration and memory can be faulty, so don't leave anything to chance. Get the exact spelling and write down the names of all specialists or facilities recommended, where they are located, and how your doctor ranks them.

If possible, request the names of your primary care physician's patients who were treated by the recommended specialists or the recommended facilities. Call those patients and find out if they were pleased with the services they received. Specifically ask what they liked, disliked, and whether they would use that provider again.

Besides your primary care doctor, you should not hesitate to contact other doctors you know. For example, ask your gynecologist, allergist, your child's pediatrician, the surgeon who operated on your mother, the hematologist whom you met at a friend's house, or the ophthalmologist who lives down the street. Get as many opinions as possible and don't worry about being a pest.

Dr. Stuart Fischer, author of *Dr. Fischer's Little Book of Big Medical Emergencies* (Barricade Books, 2002) recommends contacting the head of the relevant department at the best local hospital. For example, if you need heart surgery, get in touch with the head of the cardiac surgery department. "Department heads will usually be very helpful, even to strangers who make cold calls. They can identify the best specialists in their areas, will give you their names, and may even discuss your situation," Fischer explained.

As we stated above, contact personnel who work at hospitals and health-care facilities and fields. Nurses, interns, lab technicians, paramedics, and other staff members know which practitioners have the best reputations. They are also privy to the grapevine and may provide you with valuable insights, information, and introductions to the best.

Scour Your Network

Don't rely only on medical personnel to guide you in your search for the best health care. Put the word out to all your network partners and have them ask members of their networks. Write a script so that you can clearly tell your network contacts precisely what you need. Specifically find out if your network partners had, or know others who had, similar health problems. If they do, question them or their contacts about their experiences and solicit their recommendations. Ask if they know or have dealt with any of the specialists to whom you were referred. Fellow sufferers, even those who are complete strangers, are usually quite forthcoming with people who are facing similar problems.

You should also call your health insurance broker or agent to get recommendations. Contact anyone you or your network partners know of who works at or is involved with a local hospital or in health-related fields such as medical supplies, home health care, or laboratory services. Contact them and ask for referrals and recommendations.

Check Referrals

Double-check all recommendations. Every state has an agency charged with licensing and supervising health-care providers. Although the exact names of these agencies differ from state to state, you can get the precise names from your state's department of health. In your state, the agency that supervises physicians may be called the Department of Medical Examiners and is usually located in the state capital. Many agencies can be accessed via the Internet.

Agencies such as Departments of Medical Examiners provide the public with basic information including the practitioner's education, year of graduation, specialty, and often—and most important—whether he or she has been subject to disciplinary actions (including hospital disciplinary proceedings), felony convictions, or malpractice judgments. Similar agencies exist for other health-care fields such as dentists, chiropractors, and veterinarians and for facilities such as nursing homes and rehabilitation centers. Contact information for agencies can be obtained from local chapters of associations such as the American Hospital Association, American Medical Association, and the American Dental Association.

The American Medical Association and organizations or boards for specific specialties (American Academy of Orthopaedic Surgeons, American Board of Plastic Surgery, American College of Cardiology, etc.) are more good sources for the names of practitioners in your area. Usually, they furnish only basic information, but you can identify the leading practitioners by checking these organizations' newsletters and press releases and noting whom they select to speak and conduct workshops at their conferences, conventions, and events. Also check *www.searchpointe.com* to find whether a physician has gone through disciplinary proceedings.

Providers' quality ratings and profiles can also be found at *www.healthgrades.com*, which furnishes information on 620,000 physicians, 16,000 nursing homes, and 5,000 hospitals. Short profiles are included in *Who's Who in Medicine* (Marquis Who's Who) of practitioners who are leaders and outstanding achievers. The *Healthcare Reference Book: America's Leading Healthcare Providers and Suppliers* (Dun & Bradstreet) provides contact information on 36,000 U.S. businesses and institutions including pharmaceutical companies, medical device manufacturers, hospitals,

What You Need to Know

In your search for the best health-care provider, ask the following questions:

- Is the office/facility conveniently located?
- Does it have convenient hours?
- Is it part of a group?
- Is round-the-clock care provided? If so, by whom?
- Is the staff friendly, polite, and patient with you?
- Did they take sufficient time to answer questions?
- Did they provide clear and responsive answers?
- Is the office/facility clean and comfortable?
- Do you feel comfortable with and confident about all personnel?
- Did the office/facility feel too busy?
- How long were you kept waiting?
- Were your calls returned promptly?

laboratories, long-term care facilities, home health agencies, and hospices.

Referral Services

Many professional associations operate services to refer you to providers or facilities. The most notable is the widely advertised 1-800-DENTIST. Usually, these services give you the names of practitioners and facilities in your area, which may not be the best. However, they can be an excellent starting point on your quest for the best by educating you about your problem, providing advice, and laying out the options available.

Legal Services

Although the legal profession is highly specialized, it also has a high concentration of general practitioners—lawyers who don't have a particular specialty and handle cases in a number of legal fields. Many general practitioners, as well as some specialists, will take cases in areas in which they don't specialize. In law, learning on the job is common and attorneys have been known to venture into fields in which they're not highly skilled. In most cases, one's life isn't at risk as it can be with a doctor, but the financial exposure could be substantial.

Collect Names

If you have a lawyer whom you like, first contact him or her. If your lawyer is a specialist in another area, he or she will probably recommend an expert in the field you need. The major rub occurs when your attorney recommends another lawyer in his or her firm. At this point, the reputation of the firm is paramount.

Generally, top firms have competent attorneys manning the specialties they handle, but they may not be leading experts. Plus, firms can be weak in certain areas or want to build up those segments of their practice.

The best way to protect yourself is to ask your lawyer to recommend the three best lawyers in the field—regardless of whether they are members of his or her firm. If you decide to go with a specialist in your lawyer's firm, make sure that your lawyer agrees to be available to answer your questions and act as your liaison in dealing with the specialist.

If your lawyer is a general practitioner who wants to handle your matter, question him or her extensively on his or her experience in such matters. Find out how many similar matters he or she has successfully handled. Request specific answers and numbers and be willing to wait for the lawyer to compile the information you want. Get your lawyer to give you the names of three attorneys he or she considers the best in the field and don't let your lawyer represent you unless you feel confident that he or she will do a great job.

Using Your Network

The best way to find the best lawyer is through your network. Start with the most successful and prominent of your network partners, those who have or work for successful and/or substantial businesses. Successful people tend to rely on and be represented by the top attorneys. When your network members can't recommend a top lawyer, find out if they know others who could.

When you contact your network members, identify those who are most likely to have an entrée to the specific experts you need. For instance, if you're bogged down in a real estate dispute, call your network partners who are developers, real estate brokers, mortgage brokers, bankers, and building contractors. In most cases, they will know the best attorneys for you to call.

A Warning

When an expert represents you, an underling or paralegal will often perform much of the work. Some associates may be brilliant, tomorrow's future stars, but they can also be young, inexperienced, and overworked. Find out up front who will be working on your case, who will supervise them (and how closely), and precisely whom you can contact for information and updates. Stress that you are hiring the expert and that you expect him or her to be responsive to you. Top experts generally hire young lawyers who have the potential to be the best, and they closely supervise their performance. Most experts are vigilant about maintaining their reputations and insist upon receiving the highest quality work from their staff. However, top people also tend to be extremely busy, which can delay their returning your calls.

Bar associations and nonprofit legal organizations that focus on certain fields (the arts, immigration, civil rights, etc.) and specific groups (ethnic, gay/lesbian, AIDS patients, etc.) conduct workshops, seminars, and presentations led by experts in their fields. To get the names of the experts who appear at these events, check the organization's Web site, newsletters, calendars, and publications. Leading experts frequently teach in law schools or supervise clinics that are manned by students. The staff at law school clinics can also give you the names of the top attorneys in their fields.

Check Referrals

To find information about a lawyer, including whether he or she has been subject to disciplinary proceedings, see *www. lectlaw.com/files/att21.htm*, a directory that lists the state agencies that handle such proceedings. These agencies can tell you when the attorney was admitted to the bar, where he or she practices, contact and educational information, and whether there is a public record of disciplinary proceedings. *The Best Lawyers in America* (Woodward/White, 2000) gives the contact information for attorneys who have been voted the best by their peers.

Referral Services

Bar associations operate services that will refer you to local attorneys. If you need a specialist, they will try to connect you with someone experienced in the field. Check with the bar associations in your county or state for referral services. Like health-care services, legal referral services may not send you to the best lawyer, but they are great places to start. For a discounted fee, which is far less than you would pay most specialists, you can educate yourself and receive valuable information and advice.

Local lawyers sign up to receive referrals from the service and must go through an approval process that reviews their qualifications and experience in their specialty area. If you have a criminal law problem, a referral service will give you the name of an attorney or schedule a consultation for you with one who is experienced in criminal law. A consultation can be for thirty minutes at a special rate in the area of $25 to $50. Fees for additional time or appointments are at the attorney's usual rate. Some referral services waive the initial fee in certain matters, including personal injury, workers' compensation, and social security. Services usually assign attorneys on a rotational basis, but many try to send you to a lawyer who is experienced in the problem you face.

In addition to bar associations, other nonprofit legal organizations operate attorney referral services. These services can refer you to attorneys who specialize in a wide array of fields including art, music, literature, civil rights, landlord tenancy, immigration, and many more. For further information on these services, check with people in the industries, the local bar association, or local law schools.

Financial Services

Networking is crucial in finding the best financial assistance whether it's a tax preparer, bookkeeper, business accountant, auditor, stockbroker, or financial planner. The surest route for finding the best finance professional is word of mouth—by asking successful people you know, trust, and admire to recommend experts to you.

Start by speaking with your most financially successful network partners—people who understand the importance of financial assistance and have built great teams to help them gain and preserve their wealth. Successful businesspeople usually love to talk about finances and know the best people for you to call. Frequently, you could not reach the experts they use without their referral.

Taxes are usually the largest single expense we face during our lives (and often after our deaths) so find a great tax preparer. Tons of people prepare taxes, but don't use anyone who is not an Enrolled Agent (EA). An EA is licensed by the federal government and can appear in place of taxpayers before the Internal Revenue Service. EAs must pass a tough two-day examination administered by the IRS and an IRS background check, and they must take continuing professional education to maintain their status. To find an EA or to verify the status of your tax preparer, go to *www.naea.org* (National Association of Enrolled Agents).

Interview prospective tax preparers until you find one you have confidence in and can talk with comfortably. "It takes time to discuss a client's tax situation and to strategize," Marlena Weinstein, a top EA, points out. "So be sure your preparer gives you enough time or he or she may not get the full picture. Note how quickly the preparer grasps your situation and what creative approaches are proposed. It helps to have a reputation and relationship with the IRS because it's essential to know how audits work."

Since you want the best, find out how much of your work will be delegated and to whom. Will it be assigned to someone on staff, or someone outside the office? What are the qualifications and experience of the people who will be doing the work? Get assurance that the EA will carefully review assignments that they delegate. "Be alert for burnout," Weinstein warns. "It's endemic in the profession, especially during tax season." Tired, overworked, and burned-out people make more mistakes.

Other Financial Professionals

If you're operating a business and need a bookkeeper, auditor, or CPA, get recommendations from colleagues in your industry or a similar one. Find firms who have experience performing the precise tasks you need.

Recommendations are also crucial in hiring stockbrokers and financial advisors and planners. Again, contact the most successful members of your network. Information on investment dealers can be obtained from the National Association of Stock Dealers *(www.nasdr.com)*.

"Get recommendations from successful, older investors; they've lived through the ups and downs and understand the overall picture," suggests Ed Lefkowitz, an eminent financial advisor. "Look for someone who has at least ten years' experience and has been through at least one bear market, because you want someone who has gained respect for people's money because he or she has had the experience of losing his or her own. Make sure that your advisor will admit when he or she doesn't know an answer, push to find the best answers and delegate what he or she doesn't know to the best people."

According to Lefkowitz, a top financial advisor should, at the least, ask you:

- What are your financial objectives?
- Where do you want to be in ten years?
- Where did the money you're investing come from?
- What is your threshold of pain or risk tolerance?

Check with the National Association of Stock Dealers for further information on securities firms and financial advisors. Virtually all securities firms in the United States belong to NASD, which includes some 5,500 brokerage firms, 90,000 branch offices, and more than 650,000 registered securities representatives. Reports on brokers or brokerage firms can be accessed via NASD's Public Disclosure Program *(www.nasdr.com/2001.asp)* or by phoning 800-289-9999. Reports on brokers include disclosures on his or her experience for the past ten years, felony charges and convictions, investment-related misdemeanors and convictions, civil actions and proceedings, pending investigations, complaints and bonding company denials, payments, or revocations.

Real Estate

To find the best real estate agent or broker, turn to your network. The experience of buying or selling property can be intense and complex. It involves lots of money, long-term mortgages, as well as perplexing legal documents, terminology, and costs. Negotiations can be tense and emotions can run wild. Plus, you face the traumas of moving. So speak with your network partners about their experiences. Get the names of agents who remained pleasant and level-headed during storms, and who explained everything clearly, negotiated strongly, and looked out for their clients' best interests.

Survival of the Fittest

Real estate agents work on commission, but large commissions and sales can be infrequent. An agent's job is demanding and pressurized, it entails long hours, and the competition is fierce. As a result, the turnover is great. Mere survival is a good sign; longevity suggests that the agent is capable and successful.

Since the stakes are so high, even when you do get a glowing recommendation, check out each possible real estate agent. Contact your local Better Business Bureau and/or the Office of the Attorney General in your state to request a report on whether complaints have been filed about the agent.

If you're selling property, check with your local Board of Realtors or Realtors Association to learn who won awards for the most sales. To find the best agent, super agent Cherie Galloway Backus says, "Ask friends, family, and business connections if, in the past three years, they've worked with an agent they liked. Question enough people to get at least three names and then interview each. Ask them to bring to the interview recommendations from their clients and make sure to check them. Also request their recent listings and their marketing plan for your property. Find out how long they've been in the business and check if their company has a reputation for hiring quality people."

"Try to find out if an agent is spread too thin. Ask how many matters they're handling and how many assistants they have. Some may brag that they have fifty listings, but how many can they really handle well?" Backus points out. "Another way to find the right agent is by going to open houses and seeing agents in action. You may hit it off, like the agent's style and decide that's the one for you."

Job Hunting

Networking is an invaluable job-hunting tool because most openings, especially many high-paying senior positions, are not publicly advertised. They're filled by internal promotions, in-house transfers, personal contacts, referrals, recommendations, and word of mouth. Most employers prefer to hire people they know or those who are highly recommended by people they trust, especially when they need reliable help. Plus, personal recommendations can eliminate stiff advertising and recruitment agency costs.

Networking can give job-hunters a tremendous advantage. When the first candidates who learn about job openings move swiftly, they can sell themselves to potential employers before the competition discovers that the vacancies exist. When candidates hear about openings before employers write job specifications, they can play a role in shaping the position. In fact, with highly qualified candidates, the position can be shaped to reflect their skills.

Spread the Word

Contact former coworkers, bosses, managers—people who know your capabilities and your industry. Don't be discouraged if they've moved on and are hard to locate. Consider it a bonus, since their moving on could open up more opportunities for you.

Call contacts you've made in your industry including vendors, suppliers, and subcontractors. Also approach your friends, family, mentors, teachers, guidance counselors, and all your network members. Call people you met through alumni associations; trade, industry, and professional associations; and social, civic, charitable, and religious groups. Touch all of the bases.

Tell those you contact that you're looking for a job. Send them a copy of your resume. Give them as much information as possible on you and your goals so that they can zero in on contacts, companies, and positions that would make good fits. Tell them your areas of interest, but be clear when you're flexible and open to new directions and challenges. Ask their advice on how you should proceed and whom you should contact. Make them your partners; give them some stake in your success. When they refer you to others, obtain their permission to use their names.

Ask your network contacts if they know anyone in industries or career fields of interest whom you can call to set up informational interviews. Informational interviews are not conducted to get jobs, but are to obtain information about an industry or an occupation and to make network contacts in those areas. They are a great way to obtain information about an industry, especially for those who may want to change industries or careers. In addition, the people you interview can become important network contacts who can tip you off to openings.

The trick with informational interviews is to find people who are willing to let you interview them. The best approach is to be considerate of their time and conduct telephone or instant messenger interviews. Be professional. Keep in mind that you are trying to enlist a new member into your network who will continue to give his or her help. Write a list of questions, focus on your objectives, and don't allow the interview to meander. Ask if he or she could refer you to others whom you could interview, alert you when openings arise, and how you can help him or her.

Build network contacts with other job hunters who are looking for work in the same industry or career field. By joining forces, you can share information and contacts, look for opportunities for one another, and increase the possibilities.

Keep in Touch

Stay in touch with your network contacts and update them on your progress at each stage in which they played a part.

Thank them for their help, express your appreciation, and look for opportunities to reciprocate. Take the time to send notes and e-mail those who help you. Send gifts to those who make special efforts or when your ship comes in.

Stay in contact during the good times, when you don't need help. It's awkward and uncomfortable to reconnect when you need help and you may not get their fullest efforts. By remaining in contact when you're not in need, you will have easy access to important contacts when you do need them and they will be more willing to help.

Dating

Networking has always been an integral part of dating. How many millions of people met their sweethearts through being "fixed up" on blind dates? Introductions, referrals, and match-making are natural and time-honored practices for bringing single people together. And in this age when both women and men are swamped by busy, unrelenting, fast-track careers, dating has become a major industry.

Dating services come in every size, shape, and form. They're in most cities and all over the Internet—sites like match.com, friendster.com, and itsjustlunch.com, just to name a few. The proliferation of dating services has spawned Net directories, sites you can search to find the right dating service. They include: datingsitesguide.com, internetdating.net, and aarens.com.

An interesting trend is accelerated dating, a high-speed matchmaking technique designed to help singles quickly meet and connect with members of the opposite sex. Accelerated dating is also known by many other similar names such as speed, fast, quick, or express dating. In one evening, a single can meet and hold a number of brief, but uninterrupted, conversations with other singles who are looking to enter into romantic relationships. In many ways, these conversations are nothing more than interviews to see whether the other is worthy of another shot. Although multiple variations of accelerated dating exist, the following generally outlines how the process works:

A group of unmarried women and men gather at a restaurant, recreation center, or other meeting room to meet and talk with one another. The group can have certain common denominators such as religion, ethnic background, interests, backgrounds, and careers. The proceedings start when, at a given signal, each of the men goes to a separate table to conduct a one-on-one conversation with the woman assigned to that table for the evening. The host organizations usually suggest that the participants keep conversations light and avoid probing deeply into relationships or personal matters. Instead, they are encouraged to discuss their interests, families, and where they live. Work and career can also be discussed broadly. Typical questions include what do you like to read, what movies do you like, and what do you do on weekends. After a set time, which can vary from three to fifteen minutes, a signal sounds. The signal directs the men to move to the next table where another woman is waiting.

After each visit, both parties indicate on a form whether they would like to see that person again. At the end of the evening, the forms are collected by the host organization and correlated. If a man and woman both indicate on the form that they would like to see each other again, the host organization informs them both and gives them information for contacting each other.

Fourteen

Survey Says— Networking Do's

"When a man tells you that he got rich through hard work, ask him: 'Whose?'"

—Don Marquis, humorist

In our research for this book, we surveyed a wide range of experienced networkers to uncover what they considered the most essential requirements for successfully networking with the best people. The most frequently expressed responses are listed below. Please note that the list below does not place the responses in the order that the respondents indicated were the most important. Instead, they have been arranged to provide a logical, orderly sequence that tracks the networking process.

1. Believe that networking will work

Unless you are truly convinced your networking efforts will help you succeed, you will waste everyone's time. Networking requires a positive attitude. Positive energy translates into enthusiasm, which is contagious. The top people are usually excited about ideas. If they don't sense your excitement, they may not fully listen to you. Your belief in your cause will convince them to help you and to spread your message to others.

People sense when you are not a true believer. Savvy networkers will avoid you because they prefer to deal with those who share their faith in networking rather than wasting their time with those who do not or those who are insincere. People are usually eager to help and if they believe you, they will help.

2. Target the right audience

Approach individuals who can provide what you seek or who can direct you to those who can. Spend time carefully selecting and researching the best targets; the best people who can help you reach your goals. Then make a plan to meet them.

If you plan to join groups and/or attend events, select those that target the people you want to reach. Get involved with several different network groups because a single group may not be able to satisfy all your needs, but don't spread yourself too thin. Sample different organizations and events in order to meet a different cross-section of people, but give them a chance. Circulating your name widely and putting it in play in a number of arenas can be extremely helpful.

3. Make a strong first impression

Always put your best foot forward. You don't get a second chance to make a first impression and a bad first impression can be ruinous.

Dress appropriately for those you hope to impress. Have a great sound bite, know your stuff, and be prepared to reel it off at any time and with confidence. Have a longer description about you or your business down pat that you can quickly recite in the event you are asked about it.

4. Network with those you emulate

Don't be afraid to approach people whom you admire and who inspire you. Shoot for the top. Meeting those who have achieved your goals gives you a blueprint to learn from and follow. Aim high and seek out those who will help you develop and grow.

While shooting for the top, don't abandon your peers. They can act as sounding boards and champion your causes.

5. Talk to everyone you meet

Don't discount or overlook anyone. Be genuinely friendly. People remember your kindnesses to them and will go out of their way to reciprocate. When you give of yourself, even if it's only by talking to someone briefly, you're enhancing the possibility of building a relationship and getting something back. Develop a wide circle of friends and acquaintances from diverse fields.

6. Learn to read people

Pay close attention and become skilled at sensing people's needs. Learn to recognize who will give and who will only take. Trust your instincts and when they prove correct, increase your reliance on them. Learn to avoid those who only want to take because they will drain your time and energy.

7. Listen

Pay careful attention to what others say. Listen and observe more than talk. Listening can be an acquired skill, so work on becoming a good listener. Come away knowing one thing they like and one thing they dislike. Ask about their accomplishments before you tell them about yours. Be interested and curious. Don't take yourself too seriously, but take others very seriously.

8. Be willing to help

Give, give, give. Networking is a two-way street. Offer your help freely and generously. When others realize that you are willing to help them and how generous you are, they will be eager to help you. Always keep your contacts' needs in mind and be alert for leads for your network partners. Go the extra mile to provide something special before asking for anything in return. Remember, networking is not only about you.

"The core of networking is finding out how you can help others achieve their goals," according to Dave Sherman, who bills himself as "The Networking Guy." "The reason most people are not successful networkers is that they prospect, instead of networking. Prospecting is the process of finding people to sell your product or service to. Networking is being a valuable business and personal resource for others and EXPECTING NOTHING IN RETURN. The people that give the most will ALWAYS receive the most."

9. Be prepared

Become an expert, and be able to provide insightful answers to questions about your field. If you truly want to network with the best, prove to them that you too want to become the best. Prepare by reading everything. Decide beforehand whom you want to meet and learn everything possible about them. Carry and hand out plenty of cards and literature about you and your business.

Continue to learn, grow, and strive for success. Focus on building relationships and being rich in the resources of people. Also strive to fill the needs of others because, in time, you will reap the benefits.

10. Find common denominators

Common denominators are the thread that connects network partners. Without common interests, objectives, and values, bonds cannot be created. And without bonds, solid and meaningful networks cannot be built. Connect in your mind anything that your contacts may have in common and then build upon those similarities. Common interests, backgrounds, and experiences make ideal ice-breakers and pave the way to building deeper, more lasting relationships.

11. Bring value

Always have ideas, suggestions, and insights to share. Help the other person out first; don't wait for them to give you a lead or connection. Gain a reputation for generously giving value and you will never be alone or unappreciated.

12. Be honest, courteous, and fair

Deliver what you promise and when you can, deliver more. Don't exaggerate or claim to be what you're not. Deliver on time, call on time, and show up on time. Become known for your reliability and dependability. Show others that they can always count on you.

Always be fair and ethical; it will gain you respect, admiration, and tons of repeat business. Treat everyone with courtesy and respect and you will be treated with courtesy and respect in return. Build a great reputation. A terrific reputation is a commodity that endures, but that can be lost by just one lapse.

13. Follow up

After you first meet someone, keep in touch in a creative way. Send special notes or postcards, ones that have significance to topics you discussed. Write information about your contacts' interests on the backs of their business cards. Then send them articles or information related to their interests.

Be quick to express your gratitude. Thank people with handwritten thank-you notes, e-mails, phone calls, or gifts. Distinguish yourself by promptly expressing your thanks.

14. Keep referrers informed

As you build relationships, keep your network referrers in the loop. Let them know when you set up a meeting and fill them in on your progress. If you land a project, call them at once. And at each new step, express your thanks.

Remember that those who have helped you have a stake in the outcome of introductions or connections they made on your behalf. By keeping them informed, you will be keeping them on your team and keeping them involved, where you can draw on their help and support.

15. Look at the big picture

Try to see past the momentary, day-by-day activities that occupy your life and build toward your overall lifetime objectives. Sometimes taking nothing today will position you to gain far more tomorrow. Enlarge your perspective to see beyond the immediate and constantly re-examine your long-term goals.

Fifteen

Survey Says— Networking Don'ts

"It's not who you know, it's who knows you!"

—Jill Lublin

In our research for this book, we asked a wide range of experienced networkers what they thought were the most important things to avoid when networking. The most frequently expressed responses are listed below.

1. Don't act desperate

People prefer to associate with successful people. If they feel you're desperate they will avoid you like the plague. Most people will deal with desperate people when they have to, but when the job is done, they will run from them. So clearly communicate to your contacts that you're interested, but don't make them feel that if you don't achieve your objective you will slit your wrists.

2. Don't sell

Never enter into any networking situation with the intention of selling. Networking is not sales, it's building relationships. If you try to sell, you may foreclose the possibility of forging an importance alliance. Be patient and don't try to land a contract at the first opportunity. If you sell too early or too hard, you will scare your contacts away. Instead, concentrate on building the relationship.

3. Don't monopolize

Respect the value and short supply of other people's time. When you attend networking events or have networking opportunities, appreciate that your contacts, and those you meet, are also attending to meet people and build relationships. Learn to separate business and social occasions and act appropriately at each. A business networking event is primarily a time for business. Sure, you can socialize lightly, but if you're lonely or want to hang out with friends, attend social, not business, events.

4. Don't ask too soon

Avoid asking for help until you've developed a relationship with your contact. Most people will be put off, feel exploited, and label you as a user when you come on too quickly or strongly. Be patient. Set the stage by expressing a sincere interest in others and getting to know them. Then when the relationship has formed, it may be time to ask.

5. Don't solicit competitors

Don't ask for or expect help from those who are in direct competition with you. Be realistic and don't ask others to do what you wouldn't like to do for them. Some competitors will be friendly, even generous, but don't push them. The help you request could cost them business, so why should they help you?

6. Don't show off or brag

Nobody likes braggarts and blowhards, except their mothers, and even that isn't always so. Usually, braggarts and blowhards are only in it for themselves, which is the antithesis of the philosophy of giving that underlies networking. People may tolerate boasters for a while, but not for long. Successful people usually have a choice of whom to deal with and like most of us, steer clear of those they consider to be unpleasant, obnoxious, or too self-absorbed.

7. Don't interrupt

It's rude and turns everyone off. It tells people that you think that what you have to say is more important than what they are saying, which isn't a smart way to build relationships. Be patient and wait your turn. Most people notice and appreciate forbearance and courtesy. It builds respect, which is a great way to launch relationships.

8. Don't just talk about you

Besides irritating others, you won't learn anything by talking only about yourself. Talking only about you will make others feel that you've got such a strong involvement in yourself that you have no room for a relationship with them. Talk about yourself only when another person asks you about yourself, but make it brief. Then bring the conversation back to them. Hold your tongue or you could end up talking to yourself.

9. Don't play it by ear

Anticipate and be prepared. Try to determine beforehand the possibilities that could present themselves and be prepared. Think about the people you're likely to meet, what they may say, and the situations you could encounter. Have a killer sound bite ready to deliver along with follow-up information that they might request. Bring plenty of business cards, brochures, and writing materials.

10. Don't misrepresent yourself

The purpose of networking is to build long-lasting, mutually beneficial relationships. If you pretend to be what you're not, sooner or later you will be caught and no one will associate with you. When you pretend to be what you're not, eventually you won't be able to deliver. If you can't deliver what you promise, the relationships you build won't be reciprocal and they certainly won't be long-lasting.

11. Don't promise what you can't deliver

See above.

12. Don't pry

Be clear about what information you need, but don't ask questions about areas that seem confidential. Don't force someone to tell you, "Mind your own business." Begin by asking broad questions and then narrow the focus up until the first sign of reluctance. When you sense hesitation or reluctance, immediately back off and let the other person off the hook. Don't go where you're not wanted or you will find yourself alone.

13. Don't linger with losers and "hangers-on"

Your time is valuable and if you let them, some people will take as much of it as you allow. They latch onto you, try to take whatever they can get that could help them, and are hard to shake. Usually, they bring nothing to the table and want so much. Furthermore, they block the path for others to approach you. Some are so insistent and persistent that they force you to be harsh and blunt. They can make you feel guilty. Learn to recognize these leeches and cut them off before they completely drain you. Be polite, but also be firm or otherwise they simply won't let go.

14. Don't overextend

Select a few prime targets that you think you can realistically reach and put them on your A List. Don't shoot for everyone and everything. If you arrange to have breakfast or lunch with everyone you meet your weight will explode and your business will implode. Understand that there are limits to whom to court and what you can achieve. Be realistic, concentrate your utmost efforts on a few worthy targets, and place the rest on your B and C Lists. Keep in touch with your B List contacts by phone or e-mail.

15. Don't be discouraged

Most good things take time, patience, and work. When you try to build relationships, you are attempting to become a part of someone's life and many desirable people won't let you right in. They want to know who you are, whether you can be trusted, and whether they want to spend time or be associated with you. Success usually takes trial and error and the errors can be difficult to take. Stick with it! Find network allies who can support you in these dire moments and hang in there until you succeed.

Sixteen

Summing Up

"Concentrate all your thoughts upon the work at hand. The sun's rays do not burn until brought to a focus."

—Alexander Graham Bell

Now that you've completed this book, we want to thank you for reading it and for thinking about the information that we've provided. We know that we have covered a lot of ground, so before we sign off, we would like to summarize and briefly reiterate some of the major points that go to the heart of networking. So pardon the repetition, but we are convinced these points are so essential that they can't be stressed too often.

Follow the suggestions we made in this book and add ideas and approaches of your own. First, always think in terms of reaching the best. Identify the top people—those who can best help you reach your goals. Then carefully think through all approaches to reach them. Finally, practice implementing those approaches with your family and close friends. For example, start by listing the members of your family, friends, and your existing network and how they can best help. Train yourself to look at everyone you know or meet in terms of how they could fit into your network and help you reach the best people.

While you're practicing, remember that networking is the process of building and maintaining relationships, supportive alliances that help you and your network partners reach your goals. Goodwill and a good reputation create the foundation for a solid network. To deal with the best people you must constantly create goodwill and then build upon that goodwill to forge bonds that develop into close, meaningful relationships. It's a step-by-step process and building relationships should always be the networker's primary objective. Forging solid relationships is more important than short-term goals. Every networking effort you make should be directed to building close and enduring relationships with the best people that you can reach.

Other important things to do when networking include:

1. Focus continually on networking with the best people. Learn to identify the top people in your areas of interest.

2. Develop your own style of networking. Try different approaches until you discover what feels comfortable.

3. Create a diverse network filled with experts in a wide variety of differing supportive skills, interests, and backgrounds. Think of them as experts who are fluent in languages that you don't speak.

4. Listen and observe. If you let them speak, most people will disclose who they are, what they do, and what they need.

5. Establish that you are someone others can trust and rely on without fail. The network partners you want to be affiliated with will not recommend or extend themselves for those who do not consistently deliver the best.

6. Establish your value to your network by developing the ability to spot viable leads and opportunities for your network members and recommend good matches. The best people will notice and be impressed with your efforts on their behalf and will reciprocate.

7. Work continually to increase your own expertise. The more knowledgeable you become, the more valuable you will be to potential network partners.

8. Make clear—in your own mind and to others—exactly what you want. If you fail to precisely request what you seek, you risk getting less than you desire and you might create misunderstandings.

9. Build the best possible networking toolkit, including a killer sound bite about yourself. Never leave home without a stack of business cards, your address list, calendar, and writing materials.

10. Create a comprehensive contact organization system that keeps your records current and makes it easy for you to follow up.

One more, and perhaps most important, point to remember is this: Networking is based on giving generously and graciously. Although reciprocity is important, learn to give without expectation of return; people will notice. Don't be deterred by the fact that others may not be as giving or as generous as you—just keep on giving generously. When others notice that you give so generously, you will be acclaimed for being the best giver. Others will stand in line to deal with and simply be associated with you. They will introduce you to other great, gracious givers.

You should also realize that the fruits of networking don't come overnight; in fact, they take a lot of time. It you stick with it, though, the magic really will occur.

Afterword

While *Networking Magic* is a how-to guide for creating connections in today's busy world, Welcome Wagon, too, is a company that remains an unequaled networking force, bringing America's small businesses together with our annual 6.5 million new homeowners.

Welcome Wagon was founded in 1928 and introduced in-home visits with a basket of gifts connecting local merchants to new homeowners moving into their neighborhoods. Although today we reach new homeowners via the mailbox and the Internet (*www.welcomewagon.com*), our mission remains the same—helping people find personal and professional connections that enrich their lives.

Like Welcome Wagon, *Networking Magic* is a reflection of the times in which we live. Whether you have just moved across town or across the country, are a new homeowner or business owner, you need solid strategies to build and maintain beneficial and meaningful relationships! A book for its time, *Networking Magic* explains how to network to find the best.

—Greg Hebner, President, Welcome Wagon

Reference Materials

Recommended Reading List

Breakthrough Networking: Building Relationships That Last—Lillian D. Bjorseth (Duoforce Enterprises, 2003).

Capsules: Top 25 Tips & Creative Remedies for Women and Small Business Owners—Robyn Levin (Centerpiece Publishing, 2003) (eBook).

Conversations with Millionaires: What Millionaires Do to Get Rich, That You Never Learn About in School—Mike Litman, Jason Oman, and Robert Allen (CWM Publishing, 2001).

Crappy to Happy: Small Steps to Big Happiness NOW—Randy Peyser (Red Wheel/Weiser, 2002).

Dig Your Well Before You're Thirsty—Harvey Mackay (Currency Doubleday, 1997).

The Everything® Start Your Own Business Book: From the birth of your concept and your first deal, all you need to get your business off the ground—Rich Mintzer (Adams Media, 2002).

Get Clients Now!—C. J. Hayden (Amacom, 1999).

Guerrilla Publicity: Hundreds of Sure-Fire Tactics to Get Maximum Sales for Minimum Dollars—Jay Conrad Levinson, Rick Frishman, and Jill Lublin (Adams Media, 2002).

How to Work a Room: The Ultimate Guide to Savvy Socializing in Person and Online—Susan RoAne (Quill, 2000).

I-Power: The Secrets of Great Business in Bad Times—Martin Edelston and Marion Buhagiar (The Greenwich Institute for American Education, 1992).

Is Your Net Working: Complete Guide to Building Contacts and Career Visibility—Anne Boe and Bettie B. Youngs (John Wiley & Sons, 1989).

Knock 'Em Dead—Martin Yate (Adams Media, annual).

Learn to Power Think: A Practical Guide to Positive and Effective Decision Making—Caterina Rando (Chronicle Books, 2002).

Make Your First Million in Network Marketing: Proven Techniques You Can Use to Achieve Financial Success—Mary Christensen and Wayne Christensen (Adams Media, 2001).

Nonstop Networking: How to Improve Your Life, Luck, and Career—Andrea R. Nierenberg (Capital Books, Inc., 2002).

255

Power Networking: 59 Secrets for Personal & Professional Success, Second Edition—Donna Fisher, Sandy Vilas, and Marilyn Hermance (Bard Press, 2000).

Secrets of Savvy Networking: How to Make the Best Connections for Business and Personal Success—Susan RoAne (Audio Renaissance Tapes, 1995) (Audiotape).

Streetwise Business Tips: 200 Ways to Get Ahead in Business, Most of Which I Learned the Hard Way—Bob Adams (Adams Media, 1998).

The Smart Woman's Guide to Networking—Joyce Hadley and Betsy Sheldon (Career Press, 1995).

The Tipping Point: How Little Things Can Make a Big Difference—Malcolm Gladwell (Little, Brown & Co., 2000).

The 25 Sales Skills They Don't Teach at Business School—Stephan Schiffman (Adams Media, 2002).

The 21 Laws of Influence—Hellen Davis (Indaba Press, 2003).

Organization Listings

Achiever's Forum
www.achieversforum.com

AmSpirit Business Connections
P.O. Box 30724
Columbus, OH 43230
888-509-5323
www.amspirit.com

BNI International
199 S. Monte Vista
Suite 6
San Dimas, CA 91773
800-825-8286 *(outside Southern California)*
909-305-1811 (Fax)
909-305-1818 *(outside Southern California)*
www.bni.com

BPO Elks of the USA
2750 N. Lakeview Avenue
Chicago, IL 60614-1889
773-755-4700
773-755-4790 (Fax)
www.elks.org

Chamber of Commerce (World Directory)
www.chamberofcommerce.com

Consulting Alliance PMB 224
1275 Fourth Street
Santa Rosa, CA 95404
707-522-9634
707-575-7126 (Fax)
www.edgemastery.com

eWomenNetwork
14900 Landmark Boulevard
Suite 540
Dallas, TX 75254
972-620-9995
www.eWomenNetwork.com

Executive Moms
www.executivemoms.com

IBI Global, Inc.
200 Lime Quarry Road
Madison, AL 35758
256-774-5444
www.ibi.org

Kiwanis International
3636 Woodview Trace
Indianapolis, IN 46268-3196
317-875-8755
www.kiwanis.org

Leads Club (Ali Lassen's)
P.O. Box 279
Carlsbad, CA 92018
800-783-3761
www.leadsclub.com

LeTip International, Inc.
P.O. Box 178130
San Diego, CA 92177-9926
800-25-LETIP
858-490-2744 (Fax)
www.letip.com

Lions Clubs International
300 W 22nd Street
Oak Brook IL 60523-8842
630-571-5466
www.lionsclubs.org

*National Association of Female
    Executives*
260 Madison Avenue
3rd Floor
New York, NY 10016
www.nafe.com
800-927-6233

*National Association of Women
    Business Owners*
8405 Greensboro Drive, Suite 800
McLean, VA 22102
703-506-3268
703-506-3266 (Fax)
www.nawbo.com

Network Associates (NY)
147 Hazelwood Drive
Jericho, NY 11753
516-446-4144
516-937-5234 (Fax)
www.network-assoc.com

Network Associates (FL)
19496 Island Ct. Drive
Boca Raton, FL 33434
561-477-6626
561-477-5295 (Fax)
www.network-assoc.com

Rotary International
1560 Sherman Avenue
Evanston, IL 60201
847-866-3000
847-328-8554 or 847-328-8281 (Fax)
www.rotary.org

Shared Vision Network
10300 W. Charleston Boulevard
Suite 13-227
Las Vegas, NV 89135
702-284-5233
702-446-5565 (Fax)
www.sharedvisionnetwork.com

Soroptimist International
Two Penn Center Plaza
Suite 1000
Philadelphia, PA 19102-1883
215-557-9300
215-568-5200 (Fax)
www.soroptimist.org

Welcome Wagon
P.O. Box 1400
Westbury, NY 11590
1-800-77-WELCOME
        (1-800-779-3526)
www.welcomewagon.com

About Rick Frishman

Rick Frishman, president of Planned Television Arts since 1982, is the driving force behind PTA's exceptional growth. In 1993, PTA merged with Ruder*Finn and Rick now serves as an executive vice president at Ruder*Finn. While supervising PTA's success, he has remained one of the most powerful and energetic publicists in the media industry. Rick continues to work with many of the top editors, agents, and publishers in America, including Simon and Schuster, Random House, Harper-Collins, Pocket Books, Penguin Putnam, and Hyperion Books. Some of the authors he has worked with include: Bill Moyers, Stephen King, Caroline Kennedy, Howard Stern, President Jimmy Carter, Mark Victor Hansen, Hugh Downs, Henry Kissinger, Jack Canfield, Mitch Albom, Alan Dershowitz, Arnold Palmer, and Harvey Mackay.

Rick joined the company in 1976 after working as a producer at WOR-AM in New York City. He has a B.F.A. in acting and directing and a B.S. from Ithaca College School of Communications. Rick is a sought-after lecturer on publishing and public relations and is a member of the Public Relations Society of America (PRSA) and the National Speakers Association. He and his wife Robbi live in Long Island with their three children, Adam, Rachel, and Stephanie, and a cockapoo named Rusty.

Rick is the coauthor of *Guerrilla Marketing for Writers* with Jay Conrad Levinson and literary agent Michael Larsen (Writers Digest Books) and the coauthor of *Guerrilla Publicity* with Jay Conrad Levinson and Jill Lublin. Rick can be reached at:

Planned TV Arts

1110 Second Avenue, New York, NY 10022

Phone: (212) 593-5845

e-mail: *frishmanr@plannedtvarts.com*

Web sites: *www.plannedtvarts.com* or *www.rickfrishman.com*

About Jill Lublin

Since 1985, Jill Lublin has been CEO of the public relations strategic consulting firm Promising Promotion. She is a dynamic, sought-after international speaker on public relations, marketing, and networking.

Working with ABC, NBC, CBS, CNN, and other national media has given her great insight into what gets results in the media. She works with diverse clientele, from financial institutions and technology companies to national and international seminar leaders, nonprofit organizations, authors, entertainment professionals, and entrepreneurs. Her clients have been featured in major newspapers and national magazines, including *The Wall Street Journal, USA Today, Fast Company, Entrepreneur, Inc.,* and *Fortune Small Business,* as well as television shows such as *The Today Show, Live with Regis and Kelly,* and *Good Morning America.*

Jill is the founder of GoodNews Media, Inc., a media production and distribution company that specializes in providing positive and inspirational news and information, and she hosts its television series *GoodNews TV.* Jill also serves as the host of the nationally syndicated radio show *Do the Dream,* on which she interviews celebrities, CEOs, and extraordinary people who are achieving their dreams. Her guests have included Deepak Chopra, John Gray, Jack Canfield, and Don Miguel Ruiz.

Jill is also a member of the National Speakers Association and the National Association of Women Business Owners. Jill has authored several audio programs, including *7 Key Points to Powerful Publicity* and *Insider's Edge to Powerful Publicity*; coauthored *Guerrilla Publicity* with Jay Conrad Levinson and Rick Frishman; and authored a PR workbook, *Insider's Edge to Powerful Publicity.* Jill can be reached at:

Promising Promotion
P.O. Box 5428
Novato, CA 94948
Phone: (415) 883-5455
e-mail: *info@promisingpromotion.com*
Web site: *www.promisingpromotion.com*

Index